Contents

Plates 1-8 are between pages 52 and 53

Editors' preface

Students at school or university, and others without a university training in biology, may have the opportunity and inclination to study local natural history but lack the knowledge to do so in a confident and productive way. The books in this series offer them the information and ideas needed to plan an investigation, and the practical guidance to carry it out. They draw attention to regions on the frontiers of current knowledge where amateur studies have much to offer. We hope readers will derive as much satisfaction from their biological explorations as we have done.

Ladybirds are special. In association with WATCH, the junior wing of the Royal Society for Nature Conservation, Mike Majerus has already enlisted the help of an enormous team of ladybird recorders. Their work has produced thousands of valuable records and some exciting new discoveries, and has shown that there is a widespread and active interest in ladybird biology among children and adults throughout Britain. This book will enable those enthusiasts and others to pursue their studies of ladybird natural history much further.

Sophie Allington's illustrations are an important part of the book and an essential tool for identification. We are grateful to the Natural Environment Research Council for a grant towards their costs. Some of them also appear on a ladybird wallcard available from Richmond Publishing Co. Ltd., P.O. Box 963, Slough, SL2 3RS.

S.A.C.
R.H.L.D.

Acknowledgements

We should like to express our deepest thanks to Miss Sophie Allington who produced the splendid plates and line drawings. Many others have played a part in the production of this book and we are grateful to them all: Drs S.A. Corbet and R.H.L. Disney for their diligent and exhaustive editing; Mr R.D. Pope who gave us tremendous encouragement and help throughout the production of this book, and also allowed us access to the coccinellid collections at the British Museum (Natural History); Dr W.A. Foster who gave us access to the Crotch collection in the Cambridge University Museum of Zoology. Dr J. Muggleton and the Coccinellid Distribution Mapping Scheme helped with the ladybird distributions. Dr S.A. Henderson and Mr J.S.M. Albrecht advised us on cytological techniques and ladybird chromosome complements. Dr G.E. Rotheray read chapter 4 and made a number of useful comments. Mrs J.D. Hunt typed and corrected the manuscript. Ms G. McKenzie made editorial suggestions on the early chapters. Miss T.M.O. Harris checked the whole typescript, gave many useful suggestions, and assisted with proof reading, indexing and cross-referencing of plates, tables and references.

Finally, we must thank the members of the public who have sent us their observations and records of ladybirds, and the members of the Cambridge Ladybird Survey, particularly Heather Ireland, Helen Barfoot and Linda Burch who have contributed so much to our researches on ladybirds.

M.E.N.M.
P.W.E.K.

Naturalists' Handbooks 10

Ladybirds

MICHAEL MAJERUS
University Lecturer, Dept of Genetics
and Clare College, Camb...

Richmond Publishing Co. Ltd.

Series editors
S. A. Corbet and R. H. L. Disney
Advisory board
J. W. L. Beament, V. K. Brown,
J. A. Hammond, A. E. Stubbs

Published by The Richmond Publishing Co. Ltd.,
P.O. Box 963, Slough, SL2 3RS
Telephone Farnham Common (02814) 3104

ISBN 0 85546 267 1 Paper
ISBN 0 85546 268 X Hardcovers

Printed in Great Britain

1 Introduction

"Ladybird, ladybird, fly away home.
Your house is on fire and your children all gone.
All except one, and her name is Anne,
And she crept under the porridge pan."

1.1 Introduction

Ladybirds are among the most attractive and popular of British insects. Many species are common. They may be found in almost any habitat from sea coast to mountain top, and from city wastelands to windswept heathlands. Almost every garden will have at least one species.

There are a number of reasons for the popularity of ladybirds. Firstly, many ladybirds have bright contrasting colour patterns, although not all are red with black spots. Some are black with red spots, others are yellow and black, or maroon with cream spots. Some have stripes instead of spots and some no spots at all. Secondly, ladybirds are connected with good fortune in many myths and legends. The name 'ladybird' is itself derived from the commonest British species, the 7 spot ladybird. The lady in question is Our Lady, the Virgin Mary. The red colour is said to represent her cloak which in early paintings and sculptures was usually depicted as being red, and the seven black spots represent the seven joys and seven sorrows of Mary. Finally, most ladybirds are carnivorous. Both adults and larvae feed on aphids, which suck sap and damage many crops and garden plants. So, ladybirds are of great importance as major natural predators of these pests.

Yet, despite their usefulness and popularity, much is still unknown about the distribution, behaviour and life histories of British ladybirds.

This book aims to outline what is known about the British species, and to stress areas of scientific ignorance. We hope the book will encourage you to discover more for yourselves, particularly through your own research. This group offers great scope for original observations and experiments, and its potential in the biological control of plant pests makes new contributions to our knowledge of ladybirds even more worthwhile.

Fig. 1. The differences between ladybirds and true bugs (Hemiptera).

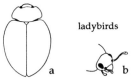

ladybirds

(a) The wing cases (elytra) meet on the centre-line, and are hard
(b) Head with biting mouthparts and with palps

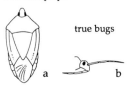

true bugs

(a) The forewings overlap, and are partly or completely membranous
(b) Head with mouthparts modified into a pointed rostrum for piercing and sucking. The rostrum usually points backwards. Lacks palps

Fig. 2. The membranous hind wing of a 7 spot ladybird.

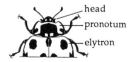

head
pronotum
elytron

Fig. 3. The position of the pronotum between the head and elytra (eyed ladybird).

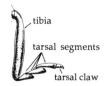

tibia

tarsal segments

tarsal claw

Fig. 4. The lower part of a leg of a ladybird showing the tibia, the four tarsal segments (note the small third segment lying almost within the second segment) and the tarsal claw.

1.2 What are ladybirds?

Ladybirds are beetles and so belong to the largest order of organisms, the Coleoptera. There are two important characteristics that, taken together, distinguish ladybirds and most beetles from insects of other orders.

(i) The forewings are modified to form hard or leathery elytra (wing cases) that meet in the centre-line, covering the abdomen.

(ii) They have biting rather than sucking mouthparts.

Beetles generally and ladybirds in particular are unlikely to be confused with any other order except the Hemiptera (true bugs). The characters which distinguish ladybirds from bugs are shown in fig. 1.

Ladybirds belong to a family of beetles called the Coccinellidae. Coccinellids are small or medium-sized beetles, 1–10mm long; they are usually round or oval. The most obvious features of the upperside of a resting ladybird are the elytra, which in most species are brightly coloured and usually patterned with spots, bands or stripes. The elytra cover and protect the membranous flight wings (fig. 2) which are usually folded under the elytra when the ladybird is not flying. Between the elytra and the head is the pronotum. This is a plate which covers the upper surface of the thorax. It is broader than it is long and it extends forwards at the margins (fig. 3). The pronotum is often patterned, though not as brightly as the elytra. The head is retractable under the pronotum and the antennae are short and clubbed. The legs are short and retractable into grooves under the body. The feet (tarsi) have four segments, but because the third segment is small and hidden inside the deeply lobed second segment, only three segments are readily visible (fig. 4).

About 3,500 species of coccinellid have been described worldwide. Forty-two are usually accepted as being British. About half a dozen other species have been recorded on one or two occasions in Britain, but they are not generally considered resident here (see chapter 7). Some of the British coccinellids are small and unspotted, and would not normally be recognised as ladybirds. This book covers the 24 species which would normally be thought of as ladybirds, although one or two of the other coccinellids are mentioned and the main key in chapter 8 covers all the British coccinellids.

Table 1 gives a complete list of British ladybirds with their common names.

Table 1. *Classification of ladybirds occurring in Britain*

Family: Coccinellidae

Sub-family	Species	Common name
Epilachninae	*Subcoccinella 24-punctata* (L.)	24 spot ladybird
Coccinellinae	*Hippodamia 13-punctata* (L.)	13 spot ladybird
	Adonia variegata (Goeze)	Adonis' ladybird
	Anisosticta 19-punctata (L.)	Water ladybird
	Aphidecta obliterata (L.)	Larch ladybird
	Micraspis 16-punctata (L.)	16 spot ladybird
	Adalia 2-punctata (L.)	2 spot ladybird
	Adalia 10-punctata (L.)	10 spot ladybird
	Coccinella 7-punctata (L.)	7 spot ladybird
	Coccinella 5-punctata (L.)	5 spot ladybird
	Coccinella 11-punctata (L.)	11 spot ladybird
	Coccinella magnifica (Redtenbacher)	Scarce 7 spot ladybird
	Coccinella hieroglyphica (L.)	Hieroglyphic ladybird
	Harmonia 4-punctata (Pontoppidan)	Cream-streaked ladybird
	Halyzia 16-guttata (L.)	Orange ladybird
	Myrrha 18-guttata (L.)	18 spot ladybird
	Psyllobora 22-punctata (L.)	22 spot ladybird
	Calvia 14-guttata (L.)	Cream-spot ladybird
	Propylea 14-punctata (L.)	14 spot ladybird
	Myzia oblongoguttata (L.)	Striped ladybird
	Anatis ocellata (L.)	Eyed ladybird
Chilocorinae	*Chilocorus renipustulatus* (Rossi)	Kidney-spot ladybird
	Chilocorus 2-pustulatus (L.)	Heather ladybird
	Exochomus 4-pustulatus (L.)	Pine ladybird

Alternative names have been used for some genera and species in the past. Some of these are commonly used in the entomological literature. Of note are: *Tytthaspis = Micraspis; distincta = magnifica; Thea = Psyllobora; Neomysia = Myzia.*

In the entomological literature the numbers in the scientific names are often given in full, e.g. *Subcoccinella 24-punctata = Subcoccinella vigintiquattuorpunctata.*

2 Life history

2.1 General life cycle

  Ladybirds pass through three stages, egg, larva and pupa, before reaching the adult state. Like all beetles, ladybirds have larvae lacking wingbuds and have a pupal stage. So, like butterflies and moths, bees, wasps and ants, and true flies, they are said to be holometabolous insects. A general life cycle scheme based on the 7 spot ladybird is shown diagrammatically in fig. 5.

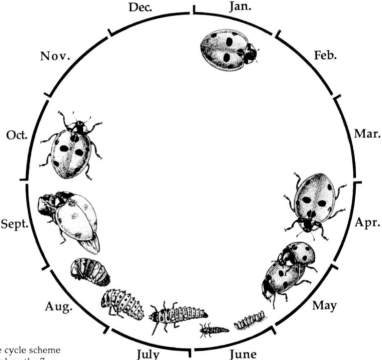

Fig. 5. General life cycle scheme of a ladybird (based on the 7 spot ladybird).

  For many ladybird species the full life cycle takes a year. Eggs are laid in spring or early summer. The larvae feed up over the next month or so, and the new generation of adults emerge from the pupae in mid to late summer. These adults feed but usually do not breed until the following spring. So most species have just one generation a year. However, there are exceptions to this pattern. The rate at which larvae feed up is greatly affected by both temperature and food availability, and the development of eggs and pupae is also affected by the climate. In some years, a number of species such as the 2 spot and 14 spot have a partial second generation. This means that individuals from both the early and late generations overwinter together. There are records of the 2 spot, 14 spot, cream-spot and eyed ladybirds surviving through a second winter. But more information is needed if we are to be sure how common these exceptions to the normal pattern are, particularly in species other than the 2 spot.

2.2 Eggs

Fig. 6. A 7 spot ladybird laying a batch of eggs.

The eggs of most species are elongate, usually oval, and they vary from a light yellow to a deep orange colour. They are laid on the leaves, stems and sometimes the bark of plants, often in the vicinity of prey. Most species fix their eggs at one end so they are found in an upright position (fig. 6), though the eggs of the pine ladybird are frequently laid on their sides. There is considerable variation in the numbers of eggs laid at one time, though most species lay batches of eggs, which are tightly packed on the substrate. Females of the 2 spot typically lay between 20 and 50 eggs at a time. There is also substantial variation within a species in the number of eggs laid per female (fecundity). One of the more important influences is the type of food eaten by the adults. Hariri (1966)* found that the 2 spot laid a total of 738 eggs per female averaging 9.3 per day when fed on the black bean aphid (*Aphis fabae*). But when the pea aphid (*Acyrthosiphon pisum*) was used, the total was 1535 eggs laid at an average of 20.4 per day. Fecundity is also affected by the quantity of food eaten, so there is a positive correlation between food consumption and egg production in the 11 spot (Ibrahim, 1955a, b). Influences on larval development also affect subsequent female fecundity. Sundby (1966) fed 7 spot larvae one third the normal amount of food and found the emerging adults were small and laid fewer eggs. It is also known that mating behaviour affects the number of eggs laid in the 2 spot. Sem'yanov (1970) showed that females increased their rate of egg laying after each mating.

Eggs take about four days to hatch, though there can be considerable variation depending to a large extent on

* References cited under the authors' names in the text appear in full in the reference list on page 96.

Fig. 7. Newly hatched larvae of the 7 spot ladybird on their eggshells.

Fig. 8. Young, first instar larva of the 2 spot ladybird, 'piggy-backing' on a pea aphid.

instar: the stage between two moults. A newly hatched ladybird larva which has not yet moulted is in the first instar

Fig. 9. Larva of the 10 spot ladybird shedding its skin to become a final instar larva.

ambient temperature. Table 2 shows that increasing ambient temperature reduces the length of time spent in the egg stage by the 7 spot, so that at 15°C it is 10.3 days, while at 35°C it is 1.8 days.

Table 2. *Development time (days) of the early stages of the 7 spot ladybird at different temperatures (data from Hodek, 1973).*

Temperature (°C)	Egg	Larva	Pupa
15	10.3	35.5	15.0
20	5.0	18.6	8.4
25.6	2.6	8.7	4.0
30	1.9	6.7	2.9
35	1.8	5.4	2.5

2.3 Larvae

When the eggs hatch, the young larvae usually remain on or near their egg shells for about a day (fig. 7). They eat the shells and very often eat those of their neighbours or any infertile eggs which have failed to hatch.

After leaving the shells, the first instar larvae must find food. They do this by actively hunting out prey. Evidence suggests that larvae discover prey by physical contact rather than scent or sight. The way the food is taken depends largely on the relative sizes of prey and predator. It is quite common to encounter a tiny first instar larva perched on the back of a relatively large aphid, as if riding 'piggy-back' (fig. 8). Its jaws are embedded into the aphid and it feeds by sucking the body fluid of the aphid. As the larva grows larger relative to the prey, it begins to eat solid parts such as the legs and antennae of the prey as well as the body fluid. Most larvae regurgitate fluid from their gut into the chewed aphid, allowing some predigestion before the aphid body fluid is sucked in.

A larva sheds its skin, or moults, three times before pupating. The old skin splits on the upperside at the front and the larva frees itself over a period of about an hour. The new skin is initially pale and soft (fig. 9) but it quickly darkens and hardens. There are four larval instars. The length of time spent as a larva depends to a large extent on environmental conditions. Prey density is important; the more prey that is available, the faster the larvae can feed and grow. Very low prey density can lead to starvation. Banks (1957) calculated that the larvae of the 14 spot die unless they find food within 1–1.5 days after hatching. If prey levels are low, but above starvation levels, then development is slower than normal. Above a certain prey density, development rate is not increased but the resulting adults are larger.

Temperature also affects development rate. In general, development is faster at higher temperatures. But this relationship is not straightforward, as is obvious from table 2. As the temperature approaches the upper tolerance level, further increases produce only small increases in development rate. So, an increase from 15°C to 20°C reduces the larval phase of the 7 spot by 16.9 days; but a similar increase from 30°C to 35°C reduces it by only 1.3 days. Still higher temperatures will retard development, or even cause death.

Fig. 10. Pre-pupa of the eyed ladybird.

2.4 Pupae

The fourth instar larva stops feeding at least 24 hours before pupation. It becomes immobile as the tip of the abdomen is attached to the substrate, usually a leaf, stem or bark. It also adopts a characteristic hunched position (fig. 10). This stage is the pre-pupa.

There are two main types of ladybird pupae. In the first, the final larval skin of the pre-pupa is shed right back to the point of attachment to the substrate, so that the pupa is naked. Most ladybird species have this type of pupa (see pl. 8.1 and 8.2). The second type is found in ladybirds of the genera *Exochomus* and *Chilocorus*, in which the skin splits lengthwise but is not shed (see pl. 8.3).

The duration of the pupal phase varies with the ambient temperature. Table 2 shows that in the 7 spot this stage lasts 15 days at 15°C but only 2.5 days at 35°C.

Pupa in normal resting position

Pupa in raised position

Fig. 11. Pupal alarm behaviour of the cream-streaked ladybird.

Although pupae are generally thought to be inactive, they are not completely immobile. If they are irritated there is an alarm response in which the fore region of the pupa is rapidly raised and lowered several times (fig. 11). This is probably a mechanism for dislodging parasites. There appears to be considerable variation among pupae as to the strength of this alarm response, and it is almost absent in some healthy pupae. There is also variation in the strength of the response throughout the life of a single pupa, though a pupa can show the response almost immediately after pupation, and until a few hours before the adult emerges.

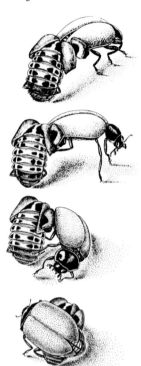

Fig. 12. Adult 2 spot ladybird emerging from the pupa and sitting on the empty pupal case.

Fig. 13. A pair of eyed ladybirds mating.

Fig. 14. Female 2 spot ladybird rejecting a male's advances by lifting her abdomen.

Pupal colouration is variable in some species. At least some of this variation is due to environmental conditions. The 7 spot produces a light orange pupa at high temperatures and a dark brown or blackish pupa at low temperatures.

2.5 Adults

The adult insect emerges by splitting the front end of the pupal case. It takes several minutes to pull itself out, and then generally rests on the empty case to expand and dry the elytra and wings (fig. 12). At this stage the wings and elytra are very soft and contain very little pigment. The colour of the elytra is best described as a very light yellow or orange. The basic adult pattern and colouration may take several hours or even days to develop, and more subtle changes take place over a longer period (pl. 4). This is most obvious in species such as the 2 spot and 7 spot that have a red background colour, which gradually deepens over the weeks and months. One consequence is that newly emerged adults are readily distinguishable from those which have overwintered, as these are a much deeper shade of red. There are two main groups of pigments in ladybirds. The dark colours are the result of melanins, and the lighter orange, red and yellow pigments are derived from carotenes.

Most adults emerge in mid to late summer. They feed, perhaps for several weeks, before dispersing to their overwintering sites.

In many species mating takes place in the spring. Ladybirds are most active in sunshine and mating pairs are a common sight in suitable habitats on warm, sunny spring days. In contrast to many insect species there is often no obvious courtship ritual. In many cases a male simply approaches a female and places his front legs on her elytra. If she accepts him he positions his genitalia and mating takes place (fig. 13). More elaborate behaviour occurs when a female rejects a male. The female may simply run away. But if a male has a strong grip on the female she may raise her abdomen (fig. 14), or kick him with her hindlegs. If this does not deter the male, then the female rolls over to dislodge him (fig. 15), or in extreme cases she climbs up a plant stem and drops to the ground. A female may reject a male's advances if she is too young to mate, has recently mated, is about to lay eggs, or has a specific mating preference for a different type of male (see chapter 6.3).

Fig.15. Female 2 spot attempting to prevent a male from mating with her by rolling onto her side.

abdomen: the hindermost of the three main body divisions of an insect

cuticle: non-cellular outer layer secreted by epidermis. In insects it is firm enough to act as a skeleton and is composed of chitin and protein

It is generally considered to be difficult to distinguish between male and female ladybirds. In most species the females are slightly larger than the males, and there may be small differences in shape, but these criteria are not totally reliable. Careful examination of the underside of the abdomen of 22 British species of ladybirds has revealed sexual differences in every case. These are best seen with a low-power dissecting microscope. Surprisingly, there is no single set of criteria that is applicable to all species, as each has its own distinctive features. These involve the size, shape and number of cuticular plates at the end of the underside of the abdomen. In some species the abdomen is pointed in the female, in others in the male, and in still others in both, or neither. The cuticular plates may be notched in the male, or undulating in the female. The only feature found in all males, and absent in all females we have examined, is three curved bands of thin flexible cuticle at the back margins of the abdominal segments. These are, for example, yellow in the eyed ladybird and glossy black in the 2 spot. They enable the abdomen of the male to be flexed at right angles during mating and hence provide a very useful diagnostic sexual feature. Figure 16 shows a representative selection of the sex differences in a variety of species.

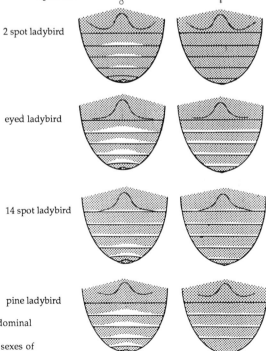

Fig. 16. Underside of abdominal segments showing the differences between the sexes of ladybirds. Males shown on the left of each pair.

3 Ladybirds in their environment

3.1 Habitat preference

Ladybirds may be found all over Britain in almost any terrestrial habitat. Some species are found in a wide range of habitats, as long as suitable food is available. Others are much more specific.

For the generalists, such as the 2 and 7 spot ladybirds, a wide variety of different aphids seem to be suitable food and enable these species to reproduce. So these ladybirds and their immature stages may be found on a wide range of plants.

The specialists tend to be found on one or a small group of host plants. At least some of these species may require food of a specific type for reproduction. The early stages of the striped ladybird are found exclusively on conifers. When adults of this species are given other species of aphids such as pea aphids, black bean aphids, or nettle aphids (*Microlophium carnosum*), they feed on them readily but will not lay eggs. The hieroglyphic ladybird seems to have a requirement for specific heather feeding prey.

One of the most habitat specific species is the water ladybird, which is almost exclusively confined to wetland areas where reed mace (*Typha latifolia*) and reeds (*Phragmites australis*) are its host plants.

Some species, although not confined to specific host plants, seem to have habitat preferences. The 11 spot is most often found in coastal areas, although it may be found inland. Adonis' ladybird seems to prefer dryish habitats, particularly on sandy soils. Both the 10 spot and cream-spot ladybirds are, in broad terms, generalists, but they will most often be met in deciduous woodland or along hedgerows. The scarce 7 spot is found in a range of habitats, but almost invariably close to nests of the wood ant, *Formica rufa* (chapter 4.3).

Table 3 gives a list of the preferred habitats of all British ladybirds. In some cases the data on which the table is based are limited, and further research and observation are needed to confirm these speculations. These cases are indicated by asterisks in the table.

Table 3. *Habitat preferences*

Species	Preferred habitats
24 spot ladybird	Grassland, meadowland.
13 spot ladybird *	Marshland.
Adonis' ladybird *	Diverse, usually on sandy soils.
Water ladybird*	*Phragmites* and *Typha* reed beds, marshlands.
Larch ladybird	Conifer woodland.
16 spot ladybird*	Grassland, meadowland.
2 spot ladybird	Diverse.
10 spot ladybird	Hedgerows, woodland.
7 spot ladybird	Diverse.
5 spot ladybird *	Unstable river shingle.
11 spot ladybird	Diverse, mainly in coastal areas.
Scarce 7 spot ladybird*	Diverse, usually near wood ants' nests.
Hieroglyphic ladybird	Heather heathland.
Cream-streaked ladybird	Conifer woodland, particularly Scots pine.
Orange ladybird *	Deciduous or coniferous woodland, particularly sycamore.
18 spot ladybird	Conifer woodland, particularly in the crowns of mature Scots pine.
22 spot ladybird	Grassland, meadowland.
Cream-spot ladybird	Hedgerows, deciduous woodland.
14 spot ladybird	Diverse.
Striped ladybird	Conifer woodland, particularly mature Scots pine.
Eyed ladybird	Conifer woodland, particularly Scots pine.
Kidney-spot ladybird *	Deciduous woodlands, mainly sallow, poplar, birch and ash.
Heather ladybird	Heather heathland, conifer scrub.
Pine ladybird	Conifer woodland, occasionally on deciduous trees.

* Habitat preferences based on relatively few records, and probably incomplete.

Some of the habitat preferences are very strong; the water, hieroglyphic and kidney-spot ladybirds will rarely be found far from their host plants. However, it must be remembered that as ladybirds can fly, all species will, at least occasionally, be found away from their expected habitats or normal host plants. This is particularly true of the conifer specialists if aphids become scarce. All of the conifer species, except the larch and 18 spot ladybirds, will readily leave their normal host trees to hunt for food on deciduous trees or lower vegetation. Some, such as the eyed ladybird, will even occasionally breed on other trees such as oak, maple and sycamore. The larch ladybird, which may be found on larch, Douglas fir and Christmas trees, as well as Scots pine, and the 18 spot, which breeds almost exclusively in the crowns of mature Scots pine, do not seem to follow this habit. Rather they either search for other conifers where aphids are more plentiful, or stay put until aphid numbers have increased.

Although the generalists may be found on a range of plants, even these have some preferences. The 2 spot is only rarely found on conifers, while the 14 spot and 7 spot often are. Indeed, in conifer habitats the 7 spot is often the most abundant ladybird.

Some of the generalists show a rather regular cycle in their movements from one host plant to another through the year. These cycles vary from one area to another and may be disrupted in some years if the aphids on one of the host plants are unusually scarce.

Table 4. *Cycle of host plants on which 2 spot ladybirds were commonly found in the Fen Causeway area of Cambridge, 1981–1986*

	1981	1982	1983	1984	1985	1986
April	-	-	H S L	-	-	-
May	L W	L W N	S L	L W B	L W	-
June	L W N	L W N	P N	L B N	L N	S L N G
July	N G	N	N	N	N	N G
August	N T	T F	N T F	N F	T N	N G C
September	T	T F	T F	F O	T F	C W T F

L - lime (*Tilia*) W - willow (*Salix*) N - nettles (*Urtica dioica*) G - long grasses T - thistles
F - fat hen (*Chenopodium*) H - hawthorn (*Crataegus*) S - sycamore (*Acer pseudoplatanus*)
P - fruit trees (*Prunus*) B - birch (*Betula*) O - oak (*Quercus*)
C - chamomile (*Matricaria* and *Tripleurospermum*)

Table 4 shows the most common host plants for the 2 spot in Cambridge for the years 1981–1986. The basic order of the cycle is fairly constant, but occasionally a regularly used plant does not support a good enough aphid population for it to be used. This was true for fat hen (*Chenopodium* species) in 1981. On other occasions the order of usage may be changed, so willows (*Salix* species) were used after nettles (*Urtica dioica*) in 1986. One or two non-regular host plants are also sometimes important, such as birch in 1984.

3.2 Alternative foods

Food that supports both complete larval development and maturation of the ovaries is described as 'essential food'. Even if they are fairly specific with respect to their essential food, many predatory species of ladybird readily accept a diverse array of alternative foods which are 'accepted but inadequate' – foods on which larval development and egg laying are prevented or reduced. Predatory ladybirds will eat a wide range of other insects if their normal food is scarce. They will also scavenge on the corpses of many invertebrate organisms, and will feed on red meat when other suitable food is not available. Indeed, ladybirds have occasionally been reported biting strongly into human skin. This was particularly true during the great 7 spot population explosion of 1976, when millions of these ladybirds, having decimated the aphid populations of southern England, made an extreme nuisance of themselves as they bit into virtually anything.

Ladybirds will also eat pollen and nectar from flowers when insect food is scarce. This allows the ladybirds to survive at least for short periods; they will then resume normal egg laying once their normal insect prey becomes available again. It may be important for ladybirds to maintain a relatively high water content, and when food is scarce, ladybirds have often been observed drinking from dew or rain drops.

3.3 Non predatory ladybirds

Four of the British ladybirds are not carnivores. The 24 spot is a true vegetarian. Both the larvae and adults of this species feed on the leaves of a variety of plants.

The 16 spot, 22 spot and orange ladybirds are all mildew feeders. The 16 spot and 22 spot are both predominantly meadow and grassland species. The 22 spot, for example, seems to favour mildews growing on the leaves of umbellifers such as hogweed (*Heracleum sphondylium*) or wild angelica (*Angelica sylvestris*).

The orange ladybird is a woodland species and feeds principally on mildews on the leaves of deciduous trees, particularly sycamore, although it will feed on honeydew and occasionally on small aphids, particularly in the spring and early summer before mildews have developed substantially on the young leaves of deciduous trees.

3.4 Overwintering

In Britain the winter is an unfavourable period for ladybirds. Lack of food and relatively low temperatures mean that this period is unsuitable for high levels of activity, so it is advantageous if this period can be passed in a more or less inactive or dormant state. All the British ladybirds pass the winter as adults. In the autumn, ladybirds which emerged from pupae in the summer will feed up and then find a suitable place to pass the winter. Most species select their winter quarters in September or early October.

Different species use different types of sites to pass the winter. Some, such as the 7 spot and 14 spot, will overwinter in almost any slightly sheltered position, in curled up leaves, or hollow plant stems close to the ground. The 2 spot usually chooses a position higher up, either exposed on tree trunks, or in cracks in or under bark. Many 2 spots are found in cracks around window frames, or actually inside buildings. Pine ladybirds usually pass the winter on Scots pine, some finding sheltered positions under bark, or in pine cones, others simply tucking themselves up in a twig joint or shoot axil. The pine ladybird seems to favour south facing overwintering sites. Conversely, the heather ladybird, when it overwinters on trees, almost invariably does so in a north facing situation. The 24 spot, 22 spot and 16 spot all usually stay close to the ground in their grassland habitats, but usually select a slightly raised piece of earth like a grass clump. Presumably this sort of situation will stay drier in particularly wet weather. The overwintering sites of some species are not known. Both the eyed ladybird and the striped ladybird are fairly common conifer species. As these are our two largest ladybirds it is surprising that their preferred winter quarters are completely unknown. Table 5 gives a list of suspected preferred overwintering sites of the British ladybirds. In many cases, the proposed sites are based on relatively few records, and work is needed to verify these speculations, and to add to the list of overwintering sites. Species which come into this category, and those species for which overwintering sites in Britain have not been recorded at all, are marked with asterisks.

Table 5. *Overwintering sites*

Species	Preferred overwintering sites
24 spot ladybird	Low herbage, grass tussocks; partially active.
13 spot ladybird *	Unknown.
Adonis' ladybird *	In plant litter in dry situations.
Water ladybird	Between leaves and in stems of *Phragmites* and *Typha* reeds, grass tussocks.
Larch ladybird	In bark crevices, usually pine.
16 spot ladybird	In plant litter, grass tussocks, fence posts in dry situations, dry stone walls; partially active.
2 spot ladybird	In buildings, on tree trunks, under bark, usually well above ground level.
10 spot ladybird	In leaf litter, plant debris, beech nuts.
7 spot ladybird	Diverse, but usually close to the ground.
5 spot ladybird *	In litter, under stones.
11 spot ladybird *	In plant litter.
Scarce 7 spot ladybird *	In gorse bushes, plant litter, bracken fronds.
Hieroglyphic ladybird *	In litter under heather.
Cream-streaked ladybird*	Under bark, in bark crevices.
Orange ladybird *	In leaf litter.
18 spot ladybird	In crowns or bark crevices of mature Scots pine.
22 spot ladybird	Diverse, close to the ground; partially active.
Cream-spot ladybird	In plant litter, bark crevices, beech nuts.
14 spot ladybird	In plant stems, leaf litter, grass tussocks.
Striped ladybird *	Unknown.
Eyed ladybird *	Unknown.
Kidney-spot ladybird *	In bark crevices or around the base of the trunks of sallows, poplars, birch.
Heather ladybird *	In litter under heather, on heather twigs, pine trees.
Pine ladybird	In leaf litter, bark crevices, pine trees.

Some species of ladybirds form aggregations during the winter. For most species these aggregations are usually small. So, although both 7 spots and pine ladybirds are found singly, they also occur in groups of up to a dozen or so. However, occasionally much larger aggregations occur. Groups of 2 spot may be as large as a thousand individuals. Large aggregations of several hundred 22 spots are sometimes found in grass tussocks. But the largest winter congregations found in Britain are of the 16 spot, in which over 10,000 have been found together.

Often aggregations will involve more than one species. 7 spots have been recorded with a range of other species including the 2 spot, 11 spot, 14 spot, 16 spot, 22 spot, larch, cream-spot and pine ladybirds. Two spots, 14 spots and 11 spots often form mixed aggregations. The larch ladybird has been found with aggregations of 18 spot and cream-streaked ladybirds. The 16 spot is often found with the 22 spot as well as the 7 spot, and many other combinations have been reported more rarely.

It is not clear how ladybirds find and join overwintering aggregations. The most likely cue seems to be a chemical scent or pheromone. It has been suggested that an odour may be released by ladybirds at their overwintering sites, and that this odour attracts other ladybirds. However, there is no experimental work to support this suggestion. If true, it appears likely from the occurrence of mixed aggregations, that the attractant scent is not species specific. Furthermore, as many sites are used by ladybirds year after year, the scent probably persists from one winter to the next.

The winter is a critical period for ladybirds, as it occupies the major part of the adult lives of most species. Most species of ladybird remain dormant or inactive for most of the winter. Mortality during this dormant period is often very high. The winter mortality rate depends on a number of factors: the dietary condition of ladybirds entering the dormant phase; the severity of the climate during the winter, particularly with respect to temperature and humidity; the timing of the onset of spring; and the availability of food as day length and temperature increase in the spring. In extremely severe winters over 90% of 2 spots may die at their overwintering sites. In milder years the mortality rate may be as low as 7%.

The ability of ladybirds to survive low temperatures also varies during the inactive period. Generally, the level of cold-resistance increases during the first few weeks of winter, so that resistance to sub-zero temperatures is rather

pheromone: chemical substance which when released or secreted by an animal influences the behaviour or development of other individuals of the same species high in the middle of winter. But the resistance declines again with the onset of spring. Hard early or late frosts can therefore lead to very high mortality.

The degree of cold-resistance also seems to vary in different species. Generally species which overwinter in leaf litter or close to the ground are more sensitive than those which overwinter in more exposed positions or in bark crevices.

Because most predatory species do not feed during the winter months, they have to survive on their food reserves. Ladybirds about to enter their overwintering sites typically show a high fat content, and the probability of survival through the winter depends, in the main, on the amount of fat that an individual has been able to accumulate before the winter (Hodek, 1973). Both stored lipids and glycogen are used as energy sources during the winter. Hariri (1966) found that about half the fat content was used up by 7 spot ladybirds between 17th September and 5th May. Smaller species used up more of their fat. In 14 spots over 70% of fat reserves were used, while in the 2 spot the usage was over 75% for both lipids and glycogen.

glycogen: a polymer built of numerous glucose molecules. Animals store carbohydrates as glycogen

lipids: substances with fat-like properties, including true fats, sterols and steroids

In some species of ladybird, ovaries will not mature until after a period of inactivity. These include the eyed, striped, kidney-spot and pine ladybirds. Other species have no such requirements, so the 2 spot, 10 spot and 14 spot will mate and lay eggs shortly after emergence from the pupa unless environmental factors such as shortening day length, falling temperatures or lack of food initiate dormancy. In still other species such as the 5 spot, 7 spot and 11 spot, the need or lack of need for a dormant period before the ovaries mature is genetically controlled (Dobrzhanskii, 1922 a, b).

Ladybirds may leave their overwintering sites in response to an increase in either day length or temperature. In some species either factor may induce the end of the inactive period.

Little is known about the requirement for an inactive or dormant winter phase in other species, or about the factors that induce its onset and termination. Investigations of the effects of a range of environmental factors on the winter behaviour of British ladybirds would certainly be worthwhile and provide useful scientific information.

4 Ladybirds and other organisms

4.1 Ladybirds as predators

Ladybirds are of considerable economic importance because most species are predatory, feeding on aphids or other plant pests. Both adults and larvae feed on the same food. Female ladybirds help their progeny to find food by laying eggs in the vicinity of aphid colonies. When moving about on plants, ladybirds do not seem to be able to detect prey at a distance, and recognise prey only after actual contact. However, the searching behaviour of ladybird larvae and adults is not completely haphazard. Hungry ladybirds tend to walk upwards because they are both attracted to light and negatively geotactic, that is they walk against the pull of gravity. Aphids show a similar behaviour, and so ladybirds will come into contact with aphids more often than they would if their movement was random. Similarly, both adults and larvae tend to walk along prominent leaf veins, and it is alongside leaf veins that many aphids feed. The searching behaviour of ladybirds also changes once a prey item has been found and consumed, for they then begin 'area restricted searching'. This involves an increase in the turning rates, and a slower rate of movement, so that a small area is intensively searched. Both adults and larvae often show side to side movements of the head, thereby increasing the area scanned for prey. This type of behaviour is obviously advantageous when searching for colonial prey where many individuals of a prey species may be found close together. If the ladybird does not find another prey item within a few minutes the turning rates and speed of movement gradually increase, and the rate of side to side movements decreases.

When a ladybird adult or larva encounters an aphid it may or may not manage to capture and eat it. Although aphids may appear to be completely helpless, they do possess a range of defence and escape mechanisms. If a ladybird approaches an aphid from the front the aphid may simply move so that the ladybird misses it. If the ladybird seizes the aphid, the aphid may kick or attempt to pull itself free. Aphids may also back away from the attacker, or drop off the plant. The likelihood of kicking, pulling, backing-off or dropping seems to vary from one species of aphid to another, but relatively little is known about the way different species of aphid defend themselves when confronted by ladybird adults or larvae, and studies in this area are needed (Evans, 1976a,b; Rotheray, 1988). Do aphids vary their defence according to the size of their attacker, or according to the species of predator? What determines whether an aphid species is a kicker, a walker, or a dropper? What happens to aphids which drop off plants? How successful are ladybirds in their attacks when faced with different defence mechanisms?

In at least one case the size of aphid seems to affect the probability of a successful attack. Older larvae of the 2 spot ladybird were successful in capturing 90–100% of first instar and 60–70% of adult peach-potato aphids (*Myzus persicae*), but only 0–50% of the much larger pea aphid (Klingauf, 1967).

siphunculus: a tubular appendage

Aphids have other defence mechanisms. If a ladybird seizes an aphid, the aphid may exude, from the tip of the siphunculi, a droplet of an oily liquid which it will dab onto the ladybird. This behaviour, which is called waxing, may induce the ladybird to release the aphid to clean itself, allowing the aphid to escape. In some species of aphid the liquid exuded from the siphunculi contains an 'alarm' pheromone. This induces other aphids in the colony to withdraw their mouthparts and walk away or drop off the plant.

Dixon (1958, 1959) found quite complex interactions between 10 spot ladybirds and the nettle aphid (*Microlophium carnosum*) (fig. 17). The response of this aphid to an adult 10 spot usually took the form of escape, whereas a 10 spot larva more often induced the aphid to exhibit a repulsion response.

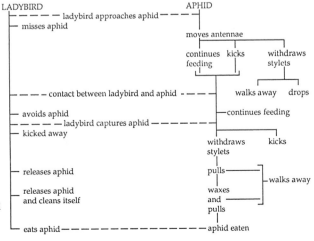

Fig. 17. The possible interactions between the 10 spot ladybird and the nettle aphid (*Microlophium carnosum*) (adapted from Dixon, 1958).

Some aphids, such as the beech aphid (*Phyllaphis fagi*) cover their bodies and surround their colony with a white flakey material. This may inconvenience predators by making individual prey selection difficult. However, the full effect of this material on predators has not been studied.

Another aphid defence is to become poisonous to ladybirds and other enemies. Larvae of the 10 spot will attack and eat both the black bean aphid and the vetch aphid (*Megoura viciae*), but after a minute or two they will reject the prey and regurgitate the gut contents (Dixon, 1958). Despite this rejection and regurgitation some larvae die as a result of this 'tasting' even when fed thereafter with suitable non-toxic food. The vetch aphid has also been shown to be poisonous to both larval and adult 2 spot ladybirds. When offered a mixture of toxic vetch aphids and non-toxic pea aphids neither larvae nor adults could differentiate between the two, and any that consumed vetch aphids died soon afterwards (Blackman, 1965, 1967).

Some species of ladybird appear to have evolved tolerance to the poisons contained in some aphids. For example, the 7 spot can feed and breed on a diet of vetch aphids. The oleander aphid (*Aphis nerii*) is poisonous to 2 spots, 7 spots and 14 spots, but is readily accepted by Adonis' ladybird which develops normally on this prey (Iperti, 1966).

A more complex problem for aphid predators is that aphid occurrence is very unpredictable. Most species of aphid change their host plants periodically. Their migration off a particular host is often induced by a deterioration in the health and quality of the foodplant, so it tends to be unpredictable. Consequently, aphid migrations can leave ladybird larvae stranded without food midway through their development.

The way in which a ladybird larva or adult eats an aphid depends to a large extent on the relative size of the predator and the prey. Small larvae generally attack small aphids, but may attack larger prey by climbing on to the prey and riding 'piggy-back' as they feed on their steed. Young larvae usually suck out the contents of the aphid, rejecting the skin and legs. Older larvae and adults may also eat some of the solid parts of the aphid, and smaller prey are consumed completely. Most ladybird adults and larvae regurgitate fluid from their gut, containing digestive enzymes, into their prey. This partially digests the prey, and the predigested food is then sucked back in. When not feeding, ladybird larvae usually rest in or near the aphid

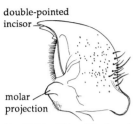

double-pointed
incisor

molar
projection

Fig. 18. Mandible of the 2 spot
ladybird, a predatory species
which feeds on aphids.

Fig. 19. Mandible of the 24 spot
ladybird, a vegetarian feeder.

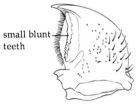

small blunt
teeth

Fig. 20. Mandible of the 16 spot
ladybird, a mildew feeder.

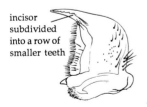

incisor
subdivided
into a row of
smaller teeth

Fig. 21. Mandible of the orange
ladybird, a mildew feeder.

colony. The adults too, usually stay close to an aphid colony when resting.

There is variation in the rate of development of ladybirds on different species of acceptable aphid. The 2 spot ladybird, for example, had faster larval development, lower mortality, and higher adult weight when fed on the pea aphid than it did on the black bean aphid (Blackman, 1967). However, the 7 spot ladybird did equally well on both prey species.

Not all predatory ladybirds feed on aphids, although most will do so if their more favoured diet is not available. The larch ladybird prefers to feed on adelgids, a group of sap-sucking insects closely related to aphids, although it will feed on aphids, such as the pea aphid and the black bean aphid, and will breed at a low rate on these prey.

In the wild, the kidney-spot and heather ladybirds both feed mainly on scale insects (coccids), although adelgids and small aphids are also eaten. In captivity both species of ladybird will breed on a diet of nettle or pea aphids, although fecundity is low.

4.2 Ladybirds as herbivores and mildew feeders

Four species of British ladybird are rarely if ever carnivorous. In the 24 spot ladybird, which feeds on leaves of a range of herbaceous plants, and the 16 spot, 22 spot and orange ladybirds which all feed on powdery mildews (moulds of the family Erysiphaceae), the mouthparts differ from those of predatory species (fig. 18). The mandibles of the 24 spot are specialized for biting off plant tissue (fig. 19). The incisor region comprises four or five blunt teeth, which carry a number of accessory teeth of various sizes. The distinct molar projection of carnivorous species is replaced by a row of coarse teeth. The mandibles of the mildew feeding species are of two types, reflecting the supposed taxonomic affinities of the three species involved. The 16 spot, which is related to the aphid eating Coccinellini, has similar mandibles to these species, but with the inner part of the mandible covered with small blunt teeth (fig. 20). In both the 22 spot and the orange ladybirds, the tip of the mandible has two teeth, the lower one subdividing into a row of smaller teeth (fig. 21).

In Britain the 24 spot appears to feed most often on campions, vetches, trefoils, chickweed and plantains, but it has been recorded feeding on other plants including grasses, and the full food plant list has still to be determined. On the continent it is occasionally a minor pest of alfalfa (lucerne).

Of the mildew feeders, the 16 spot feeds on a wide range of species of powdery mildews. The same may be true of the 22 spot and orange ladybirds. However, feeding tests using a variety of mildew species still need to be done with these species.

4.3 Predators and parasites of ladybirds

Very little is known about the predators, parasites and diseases of ladybirds in Britain. Most of the information we have has accumulated from more or less haphazard observations. But, because of the potential use of ladybirds in controlling plant pests, information about the strategies and effectiveness of the enemies of ladybirds is greatly needed, so that their effect on the beneficial activites of ladybirds can be judged.

When disturbed, ladybirds generally withdraw their legs into depressions on the abdomen, and exude a yellowish fluid. This substance, which has a bitter taste and a strong smell, gives the ladybirds some protection against many potential predators. Yet there is no doubt that ladybirds do suffer predation, perhaps principally from spiders, birds and ants. There have been numerous observations of ladybirds being attacked and eaten both by other arthropods and by vertebrates. Many species of spider find ladybirds quite acceptable, and are not deterred by the 'reflex bleeding' of a ladybird that has blundered into a web.

Records of birds preying on ladybirds have been obtained by observation and by analysis of gut contents. Most species of ladybird are at least partially repellent to birds, but birds such as swallows and swifts, which catch flying insects on the wing, do eat ladybirds. Here the ladybird has no opportunity to release its repellent fluid. Other birds have been recorded preying on ladybirds when other foods are scarce. This suggests that at least some species of ladybird are not actually poisonous, and that their distastefulness can be overcome if birds are hungry enough.

Perhaps the predators which are most often found together with ladybirds are ants. Many species of ant, particularly of the genera *Lasius* and *Formica,* attend honeydew producing aphids. These ants feed on the honeydew and give protection to the aphids. Ants seem to be more aggressive towards intruders when they are near their nest or a food source, such as a colony of aphids. El-Ziady and Kennedy (1956) showed that the ants *Lasius niger* attending the black bean aphid accelerated the rate of growth of the colony, and were aggressive towards ladybird

vertebrates: animals with a spinal column, including mammals, birds, reptiles, amphibians and fishes

arthropods: animals with a segmented body and jointed limbs; they include crustacea, spiders and scorpions, insects, millipedes and centipedes larvae, driving them away, or picking them up and dropping them over the edge of a leaf.

Ladybirds which are attacked by ants either fly away or clamp down onto the substrate if this is a flat surface. On uneven surfaces the ladybird cannot clamp down. Instead it endeavours to keep the side of the elytra being attacked in contact with the substrate. This prevents the ant gaining access to its more vulnerable undersurface. A confrontation between a ladybird and an ant rarely results in the ladybird's death. However, some ladybirds do fall prey to ants when they are attacked by several at one time. In these cases the ants may take the ladybird's corpse back to the nest.

An unusual case is that of the scarce 7 spot ladybird. Unlike other species, this ladybird is not attacked by ants, although they do react to its movement by tapping it with their antennae (Pontin, 1960). The scarce 7 spot is usually found close to nests of *Formica* species. The ladybird does not seem to rely on the ant for any basic life function. It can be bred quite easily in the laboratory in the absence of any ants. However, its immunity to attacks by ants seems to enable it to live in a niche free from other ladybirds which are driven off by the ants. The rarity of this species away from the nests of *Formica* ants suggests that it does not compete very successfully with other aphid predators.

parasites and parasitoids: insect parasites like these, that kill the host, are sometimes called parasitoids

Hymenoptera: the insect order that includes bees, wasps, ants and sawflies

Organisms known to parasitise ladybirds in Britain include two genera of flies (Diptera), six genera of parasitic wasps (Hymenoptera), one genus of mite (Acarina) and three genera of roundworms (Nematoda). Generally only larvae, pupae and adults are attacked. Egg parasites have never been recorded in Britain. This may be due to the habit of young ladybird larvae of eating any unhatched eggs. As egg parasites usually emerge from parasitised eggs after the larvae have hatched from non-parasitised eggs, the parasites themselves would be devoured before completing their development.

endoparasite: a parasite which lives inside the body of its host

Among the two-winged flies, or Diptera, the commonest species of endoparasite belong to the genus *Phalacrotophora* (Phoridae). In the South of England and East Anglia *P. fasciata* is usually the common species. Elsewhere in Britain *P. berolinensis* is more frequent. In *P. fasciata* the first segment (metatarsus) of the hind foot tends to be broader and darker than the narrower, brownish to yellowish metatarsus of *P. berolinensis*. Certain identification requires examination of the ovipositor or male genitalia (see Disney, 1983). Until 1920 *P. fasciata* and *P. berolinensis* were not distinguished and all records were given as *P. fasciata*.

ovipositor: the egg-laying
apparatus of a female insect

Fig. 22. Puparia of
Phalacrotophora fasciata which
had parasitised a kidney-spot
ladybird pupa.

Fig. 23. Puparium and adult of
Degeeria luctuosa which had
parasitised an eyed ladybird
adult.

Fig. 24. Adult *Perilitus
coccinellae*.

parthenogenesis: a form of
reproduction in which eggs
develop without having been
fertilised

P. fasciata has been recorded from the 7 spot, 2 spot, 22 spot, cream-spot, eyed, striped, heather, kidney-spot and Adonis' ladybirds; *P. berolinensis* from the 2 spot, larch, eyed, and cream-streaked ladybirds. Other host records await discovery or require confirmation.

The eggs of these parasites are laid between the legs of pre-pupae, or on the underside of newly formed pupae. The parasite larva hatches in a few hours and immediately bores into its host, where it develops, before exiting to pupate. The first sign of the effects of these parasites on ladybird pupae taken into the laboratory is usually the appearance of the dark red-brown, strongly segmented puparia (fig. 22). Several parasites may develop in a single pupa, the maximum number supportable by a pupa being dependent on its size. The 7 spot and eyed ladybirds may contain well over half a dozen parasites, while the 2 spot will rarely have more than three or four. The level of parasitisation is generally low, but may reach 50% of 2 spot or larch ladybird pupae in some populations.

The other dipteran parasite which has been recorded from ladybirds in Britain is *Degeeria luctuosa* (Tachinidae) (fig. 23). This endoparasite more usually parasitises chrysomelid beetles, but has been recorded from 10 spot and eyed ladybirds in Britain, and from a range of other species including 2 spots, 14 spots and pine ladybirds on the continent.

The eggs of the parasite are laid singly, and only one larva will develop in a host. The host is killed in the third or fourth instar when the parasite consumes its vital organs. The parasite larva emerges through the upper abdominal wall, and pupates in the soil, emerging about a week later.

Of the Hymenoptera, the most important ladybird parasite is *Perilitus coccinellae* (Braconidae, Euphorinae) (fig. 24). This wasp is exclusively a solitary, internal parasite of adult ladybirds, and it is by far the best studied of the parasites. The wasp is parthenogenetic; viable eggs are laid without fertilisation. These give rise only to females. Adult females pursue ladybirds with the abdomen flexed forward between the legs, and under the head. The female will feel the ladybird with her antennae before attempting to lay her egg with a powerful thrust of her ovipositor, through any weak point in the cuticle. The egg hatches in about five days and the larva passes through four instars. Only one parasite ever completes its development in a particular ladybird, although a number of female wasps may lay eggs in the same host. The first instar parasite larvae are equipped with grasping mandibles, with which one of the

gonad: an organ in which sex
cells are produced; a testis or an
ovary

Fig. 25. Cocoon of the parasite
Perilitus coccinellae spun
between the legs of a paralysed
7 spot ladybird.

larvae eventually destroys the others, so only one larva will
reach the second instar.

The feeding larva does not kill its host directly. It
feeds on fat reserves and on food which would normally go
to the gonads of the ladybirds which remain immature. The
vital organs are left intact.

The full grown larva emerges from the ladybird
through the membrane between the fifth and sixth, or sixth
and seventh plates on the underside of the abdomen. The
ladybird becomes virtually immobile about half an hour
before the appearance of the larva. The parasite still,
usually, does not kill its host, but leaves it partially
paralysed. The larva then spins a cocoon between the legs of
the ladybird (fig. 25), where it gains some protection from
predation from its host's warning colouration. The ladybird
usually eventually dies of starvation or fungal infection.

When the adult parasitic wasp emerges about a week
later, it already contains ripe eggs, so is able to attack other
ladybirds almost immediately.

P. coccinellae has been recorded from the 5 spot, 7
spot, 11 spot, eyed, striped, cream-spot, cream-streaked,
Adonis', and orange ladybirds. Smaller species of ladybird,
including the 2 spot, 10 spot and 14 spot, do not seem to be
suitable hosts for this parasite.

P. coccinellae may have several generations in a year,
the exact number being dependent on the weather
conditions. In cool summers there may be only a single
generation, in warm ones up to three or even four. The
parasite passes the winter as a larva inside an overwintering
ladybird.

Ladybirds are also parasitised by small chalcid
wasps of the genera *Homalotylus* and *Tetrastichus*. Three
species of *Homalotylus* parasitise coccinellids. Two of these,
H. flaminius and *H. platynaspidis*, generally parasitise only
small coccinellid species, which are not recognised as
ladybirds. *H. flaminius* is a solitary internal parasite of
coccinellids of the genera *Scymnus* and *Nephus*. *H.
platynaspidis* is a parasite of *Platynaspis luteorubra*, and
probably feeds solely on this species.

Homalotylus eytelweini is a gregarious parasite of a
number of ladybird species. Eggs are laid in the larvae,
usually when the larvae are attached to the substrate when
moulting. The parasites take only a few days to develop and
pupate inside the ladybird larva, which again attaches itself
to the substrate as though preparing to moult, but instead it
swells and the cuticle becomes hard and darkens. The adult
parasite bores a small hole in the cuticle through which it

leaves its host. The number of parasites which develop in a particular larva again depends on the size of the host, so a larva of the heather ladybird may harbour only one to three parasites, while that of a 7 spot may contain up to six. The adults, which are sexually mature when they emerge, feed on honeydew, and live for one to two weeks. They have up to four generations per year in Britain. They have been recorded from the 7 spot, 14 spot and heather ladybirds, and may use other species as hosts.

The principal ladybird parasite belonging to the genus *Tetrastichus* is *T. coccinellae*. This is a gregarious internal parasite of the larvae of a number of aphid-feeding ladybirds. Up to 25 parasites have been recorded in a single 7 spot, while in the 2 spot the average number of parasites is ten and in the heather ladybird six.

Eggs are laid in third or fourth instar larvae and occasionally in pupae. All the parasites which emerge from a host do so through a single hole. The complete development of the parasite takes three to five weeks, and there are several generations in a year.

Ladybirds are also attacked by parasitic mites (Acarina) of the genus *Podapolipus*. The parasites develop on the inside of the elytra, several females usually being present. They feed on the blood of the host and lay several hundred eggs. The nymphs fill the space between the elytra and the abdomen. The 2 spot ladybird is the most common host, but other species may also be attacked. Although the parasites do not usually kill the ladybird, they do weaken it.

Several species of nematode worm are also internal parasites of ladybirds. *Parasitylenchus coccinellinae*, which was described as a new species in 1968, lives in several species of ladybird, particularly the 14 spot. As many as 140 adult females have been found in a single ladybird, with up to 10,000 larvae and young adults. Although the nematodes are not usually fatal, they inhibit the maturation of the ovaries of the ladybirds, and also consume the food reserves of the host.

A new species of the nematode genus *Howardula* was found in adults and larvae of the 2 spot in 1965, and a species of *Mermis* has been recorded in the 7 spot, 14 spot and Adonis' ladybirds.

Very little work has been carried out on diseases of ladybirds. Protozoa of the family Gregarinidae (Sporozoa) are known to destroy intestinal cells of coccinellid larvae and adults, and may be fatal by blocking the gut with gametocysts.

gametocyst: a cyst within which sex cells are produced

Overwintering ladybirds, particularly those which are gregarious, are often infected and killed by pathogenic fungi of the genus *Beauveria*. The body cavity of a ladybird which succumbs to this disease becomes filled with a homogeneous cheese-like mass.

It is hard to assess the relative importance of predators, parasites and pathogens as causes of mortality in ladybird populations because of the paucity of our knowledge. Much further work is needed to evaluate the effects of these factors on the potential use of ladybirds as biological control agents. Studies needed include the percentage of individuals of different ladybird species that are attacked by the various species of parasite; the rate of mortality due to fungal infection in overwintering ladybirds; the effect of ladybird population density or season on parasitisation rate; the range of ladybird species which are potential hosts of parasites; and the palatability of ladybirds to a range of potential invertebrate and vertebrate predators.

The lack of knowledge of ladybird predators, parasites and pathogens means that almost any study carried out will be valuable, and there is a very real possibility that new species of ladybird parasites still await discovery.

5 Variation in ladybirds

5.1 Colours and patterns in ladybirds

Individuals of a species of ladybird often differ from one another in colour and pattern; many colour forms have been given names. For example, the commonest form of the 2 spot ladybird is called form *typica* or f. *typica*. There is a common belief that the number of spots on a ladybird indicates its age. This is a myth. In general the number of spots on a ladybird does not change once the normal pigments have been laid down in the epidermis. However, rates at which pigments are laid down do vary and so contribute to the variation seen in some species. When an adult ladybird emerges from its pupal case its elytra are soft and of a creamy, yellow or orange colour. The distinctive colour patterns soon begin to appear. Plates 4.1–3 show the colours of the typical form of the 2 spot ladybird 30 minutes, 12 hours and 48 hours after emergence. Similarly the eyed ladybird is cream-yellow, both on the elytra and on the underside of the abdomen, when it first emerges. The reddish-brown colour begins to appear within the first 24 hours, together with the black spots, and the underside of the abdomen darkens considerably. The cream rings begin to appear on the second day. A week after emerging from the pupa the ladybird is a rich reddish brown with sharply defined black spots surrounded by bright, cream rings. However, pigments continue to be laid down so that the insect gradually becomes darker during the rest of its adult life. This can be seen if autumn and spring samples are compared.

epidermis: outermost layer of cells. In insects it is one cell thick and secretes a cuticle

The rate of pigment development is variable in some species. The melanic form of the 10 spot ladybird is black with bright red shoulder flashes in its final form. After emergence, the ladybirds pass through a period when the elytra are a darkening maroon or brown and the shoulder flashes are yellow or orange before the final colours are achieved. This transition may take anything from a day to several months. Similar variation in the rate of pigment development contributes to the range of ground and marking colours in the *decempustulata* form of the 10 spot (see chapter 5.3).

melanic: dark or black

In black ladybirds sporting a pattern of red spots the elytra may first be flushed with red pigment all over before the darker pigments are laid down over specific areas. This transition is very rapid in the heather and pine ladybirds, which achieve their full colour within 24–48 hours of emergence. In melanic forms of the 2 spot the process is slower, and the order in which melanic pigments are laid down over particular areas can be studied. Plates 4.4–9 show the development of black pigment over the first 48 hours after emergence of the *quadrimaculata* form of the 2 spot.*

The changes in pattern, due to variations in the rate of pigment development, can make it hard to quantify the frequencies of different forms of a species in a population. For example, black pigment may be laid down over the hindermost pair of red spots of the *sexpustulata* pattern of the 2 spot (pl. 5.2), as much as three months after emergence. This effectively converts the form from *sexpustulata* to *quadrimaculata* (pl. 2.8). Consequently, if a significant proportion of the melanics in a population are of this type an increase in the proportion of *quadrimaculata* and a decrease in the proportion of *sexpustulata* may be expected as a new generation ages, and changes in the frequency of these forms between autumn and spring may be due to pigment deposition rather than other factors such as different chances of survival through the winter.

The rates of pigment development and variations in the rates and the order in which different components of the patterns become apparent have only been studied in a few species. Others await attention, including all the yellow and black species and some of the species having the most complex patterns such as the cream-streaked ladybird.

---

*The nomenclature of ladybird colour forms is very complex. This is largely due to a German entomologist named Mader, who described and catalogued all the varieties of European ladybirds he could discover (see Mader, 1926–37). In many cases, individuals which differ in pattern by only very minute details are afforded different names. Were we to follow Mader's nomenclature to the letter, this section would end up as nothing more than a long list of Latin names. This seems unnecessary, particularly as many of the forms listed by Mader are rare or absent in Britain. For example while he lists 119 different pattern forms of the 10 spot, most British populations consist of only three main forms, with minor variations of each (see chapter 5.3). In addition we have discovered a number of forms in Britain which were not known to Mader. In this chapter and chapter 6, we follow Mader's nomenclature only when strictly applicable. When we discuss group forms, all of which have some basic feature in common, we will either define the group by description or apply an adjectival name to the group, rather than listing all the forms which fall into the group.

5.2 Colour pattern variation in the 2 spot

One of the surprising features of ladybirds is that some species are very variable in colour and pattern, while others are relatively uniform. The 7 spot, cream-spot and kidney-spot ladybirds vary little. On the other hand, the 10 spot, hieroglyphic and cream-streaked ladybirds all have a considerable range of forms.

In some species a number of distinct forms occur. For example, in the hieroglyphic ladybird three main forms are common (pl. 3.7–8 and pl. 6.12). In others, such as the 14 spot, the variation seems to be more or less continuous, so that no distinct classes can be defined.

The factors which produce this variation are unknown in many species, although it is suspected that much of the variation is under genetic control.

genetic: concerned with or controlled by genes which enable characteristics to be passed from one generation to the next

One of the most variable of the British ladybirds is the 2 spot. In this species over a hundred different colour patterns have been described, ranging from all red to all black. The variation is most obvious on the elytra, but the black markings on the basically white pronotum also vary considerably.

In Britain over a dozen genetically distinct forms have been identified. The commonest form is red with a single black spot on each elytron. However, in many populations melanic forms in which the elytra are black with either four (f. *quadrimaculata,* pl. 2.8) or six (f. *sexpustulata* pl. 5.2) red spots are common, and a third melanic form with just two red spots (f. *sublunata,* pl. 5.1) occurs more rarely.

The range of black patterns on a red background is even greater. The two black spots present in the typical form (f. *typica*) may be extended slightly or greatly. In some individuals there are simply small extensions, either towards the centre line or towards the outer margin, while in others these extensions may spread both forward and backwards so that there are roughly equal areas of red and black. Although the range of patterns is extreme, a number of discrete patterns occur. These include f. extreme *annulata* (pl. 5.6) which is similar to *sexpustulata* but has larger red spots and a thin streak of red running backwards from the shoulder patch. Form *duodecempustulata* (pl. 5.7) has a chequer pattern of black on red; 'spotty' (pl. 5.9) has a set of eight or nine small and generally discrete black spots on each red elytron, and 'strong spotty' (pl. 5.10) is similar but has the spots enlarged and fused.

gene: an hereditary factor or heritable unit which can transmit a characteristic from one generation to the next. Composed of DNA and usually situated in the thread-like chromosomes in the nucleus

alleles: forms of a gene. Genes are considered alleles of each other when they occur in the same positions on the members of a chromosome pair, have different effects in respect of a particular characteristic, and can mutate one to another. Not more than two alleles at any gene locus can be present in a normal ladybird cell

dominant: the stronger of a pair of alleles, expressed as fully when present in a single dose as it is when present in a double dose

recessive: the opposite of dominant. A recessive allele is not expressed when present in single dose, but only when in double dose

modifier genes: a series of genes each with small effects which modify the exact expression of a major gene

heterozygote: an individual which has inherited two different alleles of the gene in question, one from each parent

homozygote: an individual which has inherited two similar alleles, one from each parent

Fig. 26. Black form of the 2 spot ladybird.

The genetic relationships between many of these forms have been studied by looking at the progeny produced by particular pairs (Majerus and others, unpublished).

A single pair of alleles controls the three melanic forms *sublunata*, *quadrimaculata* and *sexpustulata*, and the *typica* form. The dominant allele of this main colour pattern gene produces the melanic form and the recessive allele produces *typica*. The differences between the three melanic forms are produced by modifier genes which slightly alter the basic melanic pattern.

Extreme *annulata*, *duodecempustulata*, spotty and strong spotty are each controlled by a different allele of the main colour pattern gene. All these alleles are recessive to the melanic allele. The dominance relationships between these four alleles and the *typica* allele are complicated. The *typica*, spotty and strong spotty alleles are in general dominant to the *duodecempustulata* allele, although occasionally heterozygotes are slightly affected by the presence of the *duodecempustulata* allele. The *typica* allele is also more or less dominant to spotty. However, the heterozygote combination of a *typica* and a strong spotty allele produces a form called 'semi-spotty'. The extreme *annulata* allele shows no dominance with any of these forms. With *typica*, extreme *annulata* gives a range of intermediates from 'weak *annulata*' (pl. 5.3) through 'bar *annulata*' (pl. 5.4) to 'intermediate *annulata*' (pl. 5.5). Extreme *annulata* and either spotty or strong spotty produce a heterozygote called 'zigzag spotty'. The heterozygote between *duodecempustulata* and extreme *annulata* is a form called 'new *duodecempustulata*' (pl. 5.8). Thus much of the colour pattern variation is controlled by different alleles of a single gene.

Other genes may also affect the colour or pattern. The recessive allele of another gene, when present with the spotty homozygote, modifies the spotty form to produce a form called '*sexpustulata* spotty' (pl. 5.11) which appears intermediate between *sexpustulata* and extreme *annulata*. This allele, which seems to increase the amount of black patterning, also modifies the extreme *annulata* form, to a form called 'melanic *annulata*' (pl. 5.12) which has almost as much black as *quadrimaculata*. The recessive allele of a third gene can modify melanic *annulata* or strong spotty to produce a form that is almost completely black (fig. 26).

The rate of deposition of red pigment varies amongst the forms of the 2 spot. Red pigment appears sooner in the melanics and the typical form than it does in the other forms. In *duodecempustulata* and spotty, the ground colour may still be a relatively pale orange a month after emergence from the pupa. In addition, the orange and red pigments seem to be laid down at different rates in different regions of the elytra, giving the ladybirds a rather streaky appearance. Very occasionally the basic ground colour may be very different indeed. In the form *purpurea*, the final colour of the adult is dark purple. This pigment is laid down over a number of weeks. The insect appears normal when it first emerges from the pupa. The first evidence of abnormality occurs two or three days later when the normal red ground colour begins to look somewhat dirty, as darker pigment begins to appear. This form is again controlled by a single recessive gene (Majerus and others, 1987).

Although a certain amount of work has been carried out on the inheritance of colour pattern variation in the 2 spot ladybird, there is still plenty of scope for further work. New undescribed forms are still being discovered. The genetic relationships between many of the forms still have to be determined. Also the effect of environmental factors such as temperature and food availability on pigment deposition and pattern still needs to be investigated. In addition the question of why the 2 spot shows so much natural variation needs to be addressed (see chapter 6).

5.3 Colour pattern variation in the 10 spot

The 2 spot ladybird is not the only species to show substantial genetic variation. Its closest British relative, the 10 spot ladybird, also boasts considerable variation in pattern and colour. In the 10 spot there are three main forms. Form *decempunctata* (pl. 2.10) is generally the commonest. It is usually a shade of orange, brown or tan, with small black, dark brown, or reddish spots on the elytra. The number of spots varies from 0 to 12, although very rarely higher spot numbers have been recorded. Form *decempustulata* (pl. 2.11) has a chequered pattern, not unlike the *duodecempustulata* form of the 2 spot. However, the pattern may comprise a black or brown grid on a yellow, orange or red background. There is also some variation in the width and strength of the grid, giving some individuals a much coarser pattern than others. There are reports of *decempustulata*-like 10 spots which have a pale grid on a dark background (Moon, 1986), but we have never come across any of this type, and their existence has yet to be substantiated. The third main form is *bimaculata* (pl. 2.12), a melanic form with just two pale flashes, one at the side of the base of each elytron. The ground colour varies from mid-maroon to black, and the flash from yellow to red. In this form particularly the variation in colour seems to depend on age. Younger individuals are most commonly maroon with yellow shoulder flashes; older ones are black with red.

There have been reports that the three main forms are genetically controlled by three different alleles of the same gene, and that *decempunctata* is dominant to *decempustulata* which in turn is dominant to *bimaculata*. However, recent work has shown that the inheritance is not so simple (Majerus and others, unpublished). For example, two different alleles control f. *decempunctata*. One, the top dominant, produces the *decempunctata* form in which the number of dots varies under polygenic control. This means that if two ladybirds each with 8 spots mate, the majority of progeny will have 8 spots, but some will have 6 or 10 and a few will even have 4 or 12. However, another allele, recessive to the *decempunctata* allele, produces a form which is basically the *decempunctata* form but it always has precisely 12 spots (pl. 6.10). This form is called *duodecempunctata*, and the allele controlling it T^{12}. If two f. *duodecempunctata* mate, there is no spread in the number of spots in the progeny – all will have 12. Unfortunately, f. *decempunctata* with 12 spots and f. *duodecempunctata* are not visibly distinguishable, their genetic differences being revealed only by carefully controlled breeding experiments.

polygenic: a character controlled polygenically is affected by a large number of genes each of which has a small effect

The *decempustulata* and *bimaculata* forms do appear to be controlled by two further alleles of the same gene as *decempunctata* and *duodecempunctata*, but in these there is a considerable variation with respect to colour and the rate of pigment development. This variation appears to be genetic, but it is not clear whether it is controlled by a range of alleles of a single gene or by one or more other genes. The full picture in respect of the inheritance of colour pattern variation in the 10 spot still has to be resolved. This can only be done by a series of carefully designed and controlled breeding experiments.

Forms intermediate between the three main classes do occur, but only rarely, perhaps as a result of matings between individuals which have originated in different populations. There is evidence in both the 2 spot and 10 spot ladybirds that the pattern stability of the commonest forms and the dominance relationships between the alleles controlling them are the products of modifier genes, which vary between populations. When individuals from different populations, which have different sets of modifier genes, are crossed, the genetic dominance between forms and the general stability of the main patterns may break down, producing a wide range of intermediate individuals.

5.4. Colour pattern variation in other species

Variation in the colour and patterns on the pronotum and elytra is not confined to ladybirds of the genus *Adalia*. Indeed, all the British ladybirds show some variation. There are five main components of the colour patterns: ground colour, colour of markings, number of spots, strength of spots, and fusions between the spots. All these components show variation in some species. In a few species the variation is even more complex. In the eyed ladybird the compound nature of the markings – black spots surrounded by cream rings – means that there is variation in both the presence of the rings and the spots.

The range of variation in European ladybirds was described by Mader (1926-37). However, many species vary much less in Britain than in their range as a whole. For example, Mader describes forms of the 5 spot ladybird with anything from one to 11 spots, but all known British specimens have either five or seven. Similarly, in the water ladybird, he described spot numbers from zero to 21, but all British individuals we have examined have had at least 15 spots.

Table 6 outlines the variation found in Britain with respect to ground colour, marking colour, spot number, strength of spot, and fusions between spots. Many species have forms that are almost, or completely, black, and the existence and approximate commonness of these melanic forms is also indicated.

A detailed discussion of all the minute variation in all the British species is outside the scope of this book. However, it is worth mentioning a few particular cases to illustrate certain facets of variability, and to indicate examples suitable for genetic analysis of the variation.

In the eyed ladybird, forms with cream spots but lacking the black centres to the spots (pl. 6.2) are found occasionally in the wild. There is evidence that the basis of this 'blind' form is genetic, but the precise mode of inheritance has not been worked out.

The hieroglyphic ladybird has three main forms. The most common of these has a tan colour, usually with five black spots (pl. 3.7). There is also a black form (f. *areata*) (pl. 3.8), and a form intermediate between the tan and black forms (pl. 6.12). It is tempting to think that the three forms may be controlled by two alleles of a single gene, with the

Table 6. *Components of colour and pattern variation in British ladybirds (for* Adalia *species see chapters 5.2 and 5.3). These notes have been compiled from British specimens only; many species show other variations in Continental populations*

Species	Ground colour	Spot colour	Spot number Range	Commonest	Variation in strength of spots	Fusions between spots	Fully melanic form
24 spot	Russet or very rarely buff	Black or very rarely yellow	0 - 26	20	Considerable	Common, may be considerable	f.nigra (rare)
13 spot	Red	Black	7 - 15	13	Slight	Rare, but may be considerable	f.borealis (very rare)
Adonis'	Red	Black	3 - 15	7	Slight	May be considerable	None
Water	Buff with reddish or yellowish tinge	Black	15 - 21	19	Considerable	Not uncommon, may be considerable	None
Larch	Pink, pale tan, orange, brown or mid-tan	Black	0 - 6	0	Considerable	Rare, but may be considerable	f.fumata (dark brown) (rare)
16 spot	Creamy-buff	Black	16 - 18	16 (3 lateral spots fused)	Slight	Common, may be considerable	f.poweri (uncommon)
7 spot	Red	Black	0 - 9	7	Considerable	Very rare	f.anthrax (rare)
Scarce 7 spot	Red	Black	5 - 11	7	Slight	Thin fusion lines may occur very rare	None
5 spot	Red	Black	5 - 7	5	Some	Variable	None
11 spot	Red	Black rarely with yellow rings	7 - 11	11	Considerable	Some, uncommon	None
Hieroglyphic	Brown	Black (stripes and spots)	0 - 7	5	Considerable	Considerable common	f.areata (common)
Cream-streaked	Pink, salmon or orange	Black	4 - 16	4 or 16	Some	Considerable, uncommon	f.Haneli (rare)
Cream-spot	Maroon-brown or very rarely black	Cream	14	14	Little	Rare, slight	f.nigripennis (rare)
14 spot	Yellow or black	Black or yellow	4 - 14	14	Very variable	Considerable, very common	f.merkeri (rare)
Striped	Chestnut or rarely dark brown	Cream stripes, rarely with black inside	0 - 15	13	Some	Common, may be considerable	f.lignicolor f.conjunct (both rare)
Eyed	Russet red or burgundy red	Black often with cream rings	0 - 22	18	Considerable	Rare, but may be considerable	f.hebraea (very rare)
22 spot	Yellow	Black	20 - 22	22	Little	Little, rare	None
Orange	Orange	White or creamy-yellow	12 or 16	16	Little	None	None
18 spot	Maroon	Cream or pale buff	14 or 18	18	Some	Some, common	None
Kidney-spot	Black	Orange or red	2	2	Some	None	None
Heather	Black	Red	2 - 6	6	Little	Some, common	None
Pine	Black	Red	2 - 4	4	Some	None	None

intermediate form being heterozygous. However, as the intermediate form is almost always rarer than either of the others, this explanation is unlikely. Indeed, there is as yet no evidence to indicate whether the variation is genetic or environmental.

In Britain the cream-streaked ladybird usually has either 16 spots (pl. 1.8), or only the two outermost spots on the edge of each elytron (pl. 1.7). As with the blind form of the eyed ladybird, there are indications that the difference between these forms is genetic, but again the exact mechanism is not known. This species also has a dark form in which the black spots are enlarged and diffuse at the edges (pl. 6.5). It is known that this form is controlled by a single Mendelian gene, but whether it is dominant or recessive to the normal forms has not been analysed.

Mendelian gene: a gene which behaves in accordance with the laws of inheritance discovered by Gregor Mendel

In species where some aspect of the variation is apparently continuous, as with the strength of the black markings of the 14 spot, there is considerable scope for research. The most probable explanation for this type of variation is that many genes, each with small effect, influence the patterning. If this is so, selecting the darkest individuals from a large sample for breeding should lead to an average increase in amounts of black in the next generation. If this is done repeatedly for three or four generations, it should be possible to produce ladybirds which are very much blacker than any in the original sample. As long as the rearing of ladybirds is always carried out under similar conditions, such a result would be good evidence that the black patterning in this species is controlled polygenically. It is possible that the strength of markings in the 18 spot and 24 spot ladybirds is also under polygenic control, but similar selective breeding experiments are needed to confirm this suggestion.

Adonis' ladybird exhibits considerable variation in spot number, as shown by counts for a series of samples from a Staffordshire population between 1985 and 1987 (table 7). Spot number ranged from three to 15. Most individuals had seven or nine spots. This distribution of spot numbers, with the low and high values rare and the medium values common, is suggestive of polygenic inheritance, but again, breeding experiments are needed to confirm this.

Not all colour and pattern variation is controlled genetically. As mentioned in sections 5.2 and 5.3, age may affect the ground colour and the strength of the spots. Also environmental factors, such as temperature or food, can probably influence colour and pattern. However, virtually no work has been carried out on the influence of such factors.

Fig. 27. Unusual form of the 2 spot ladybird with the hindpart of both elytra being purple.

Table 7. *Variation in spot number in Adonis' ladybird in a series of samples from a Staffordshire population recorded during 1985, 1986 and 1987*

Spot number	Number of ladybirds	% of total
3	3	1.9
5	10	6.4
7	61	39.1
8*	1	0.6
9	49	31.4
10*	1	0.6
11	18	11.5
13	12	7.7
15	1	0.6
Total	156	

* Occasionally there is asymmetry between the number of spots on the two elytra of a particular ladybird. The 8 and 10 spotted individuals are a product of such asymmetry. In each case one elytron has one spot fewer than the other.

Fig. 28. Bilateral mosaic 7 spot ladybird, with the left elytron red, and the right elytron brown.

Occasionally, ladybirds are found with very unusual markings. Figure 27 shows a typical 2 spot with a dark patch covering the hind part of the elytra. Figure 28 shows a 7 spot in which the normal red pigment is replaced by brown pigment on the right elytron, the left elytron being normal. In some 7 spots the larger part of both elytra have normal red pigments with just a small patch being brown. Figure 29 is an asymmetric 14 spot ladybird with much bolder black markings on the right elytron than on the left. The causes of such oddities are not known. In each of the three examples shown, the ladybirds were mated to normal individuals and resulting progeny were allowed to breed, yet in none of them did the unusual patterns recur in the progeny of either the first or second generation, suggesting that these pattern variations are not inherited. They may be due to disruption in pigment production resulting from injury to larvae or pupae, or to mitotic mutation in early development. Such suggestions can only be speculative until more is known of the biochemistry of pigment production and deposition.

Fig. 29. Asymmetrical 14 spot ladybird, the markings on the left elytron being less pronounced than those on the right.

5.5 Other morphological variation

mitosis: the normal process of cell division in growth, involving the duplication of chromosomes, and the division of the nucleus into two, each with an identical complement of chromosomes to the original cell

mutation: a sudden change in the genetic material controlling a particular character or characters of an organism. Such a change may be due to a change in the number of chromosomes, to an alteration in the structure of a chromosome, or to a chemical or physical change in an individual gene

Elytra colour and pattern are not the only characteristics that vary. For example, some species show great variation in size. This is usually a reflection of variation in environmental factors such as food availability or temperature. Perhaps one of the most surprising features that is subject to variation involves the structure of the elytra or wings. For example, in the 2 spot, the elytra and wings may be reduced to miniature stumps (fig. 30). This is very rare, but does occur naturally and appears to be controlled by a recessive allele.

The wings are also involved in a most unusual type of variation in the 24 spot ladybird. In the majority of individuals of this species found in Britain, the flight wings are fused together and reduced in size, making them quite useless as flight organs. The frequency of this flightless form decreases further east in Europe and Asia.

Fig. 30. A 2 spot ladybird with stunted elytra and wings.

6 Population and evolutionary biology

6.1 Population size

Female ladybirds have the capacity to lay over a thousand eggs each, so, theoretically at least, ladybird populations could increase 500 fold each generation. In fact this potential is rarely realised. Many factors can affect population size. Ladybird mating and egg laying are affected by temperature, sunshine and rainfall. The number of eggs laid by a female is determined by the ease of finding or being found by a male, the condition of the female particularly with respect to her past diet, and the climate. Not all the eggs that are laid will hatch. Some are infertile. The level of infertility is affected by the time since the female last mated, and by the age and condition of both parents, especially the female. Even some fertile eggs will fail to hatch. They may fall foul of some mishap, or they may be eaten, for although egg-parasitism has not been recorded amongst ladybirds in Britain, ladybird eggs are preyed upon by a variety of invertebrate predators, particularly lacewing larvae, and ladybird larvae and adults. Of the larvae which do hatch, only a small proportion attain the adult state. Mortality during the larval and pupal stages may be due to starvation, parasitism, disease, predation, cannibalism or any number of accidents. When the ladybirds finally emerge from their pupae, most species need to build up food reserves before the winter. Their chances of survival over this period depend on the state of these reserves, coupled with the winter climate, and the overwintering quarters found by the ladybird.

So, a great many factors influence ladybird population numbers. Occasionally, favourable conditions lead to enormous population explosions. Large numbers of aphids, together with favourable climatic conditions during both summer and winter, may permit the high potential fecundity of females to be realised. In Britain such conditions were widespread in 1975 and 1976. The long warm summer of 1975, followed by a mild winter, led to huge populations of aphids in the spring of 1976. The ladybird populations, particularly of 7 spots, 2 spots and 14 spots, began to increase during 1975, and mortality over the winter of 1975–76 was lower than usual. Ladybirds emerging from their overwintering sites were faced with an abundance of aphids and optimum weather conditions for mating and egglaying. Their larvae found abundant food, and in the hot weather of 1976 completed their development rapidly. Larval and pupal mortality were therefore low, so enormous numbers of ladybirds attained the adult state in mid-summer 1976. At the same time, aphid populations decreased dramatically, partly because of predation by ladybirds and their larvae, and partly because the hot dry conditions adversely affected the plants upon which the aphids were feeding. When short of food ladybirds become very mobile. On hot days huge numbers may take to the air, where air currents may carry them for considerable distances. In 1976 enormous numbers of ladybirds were recorded across southern and eastern Britain. Most of them were 7 spots, but there were also good numbers of 2 spots and 14 spots and smaller numbers of 10 spots and 11 spots. The numbers were greatest along the south and east coasts. Tide-lines consisted almost entirely of millions of dead ladybirds for mile after mile, and live ladybirds became a serious nuisance to holiday makers in seaside resorts. There were many reports of ladybirds biting or stinging people. In fact ladybirds cannot sting, and in normal circumstances will not bite people. The explanation of the reports in 1976 is that the starving ladybirds were biting into anything they landed on to test if it was edible, and injecting a tiny amount of digestive enzyme at each bite. When such foreign enzymes react with the body's chemical defences a stinging sensation is produced.

The enormous numbers of ladybirds recorded along the south and east coasts in 1976 led to a general belief that there had been a massive migration of ladybirds into Britain from the Continent. This was not so. The ladybirds had simply migrated in search of food, from populations spread across Britain, until their dispersal was arrested by the coast.

There have been other reports of similar explosions in 7 spot numbers. In 1952 millions of 7 spots appeared on the east coast. Again the tide-line was reported to be coloured pink by the dead ladybirds. Cannibalism was said to be rife; resting ladybirds could attack those that were landing before these gained protection by folding their wings.

A population explosion, like that of 1976, is usually followed by a population crash due to starvation, high levels of cannibalism, and often to an increase in parasite populations. It may then take several seasons for the balance between aphids, ladybirds and ladybird parasites to stabilise again. Generally, these occasional population explosions involve only the aphid- or adelgid-feeding species. This suggests that they depend on the occasional, exceptional abundance of prey. Explosions are almost unknown in vegetarian, mildew-feeding or scale insect-preying species, whose food supply tends to fluctuate less (Hodek, 1973).

Although many factors are known to affect ladybird abundance, the relative importance of different factors has rarely been studied, and almost any carefully conducted population study is likely to produce useful and novel information. For example, studies might investigate the incidence of the different types of parasite, or how cannibalism is related to population density. Mortality over the winter period could be investigated by carrying out mark-release-recapture experiments (see chapter 9) in the autumn and spring. Ladybird migrations also need to be studied. We know ladybirds move in search of food, and they also migrate to and from overwintering sites, but we know little about the distances which ladybirds may move from one generation to the next. Information of this type is particularly important if we are to understand the factors which determine the frequencies of forms of a species in different populations (see chapter 6.3).

6.2 Warning colouration

Most ladybirds sport two or more bright contrasting colours. These are thought to warn potential predators that ladybirds are distasteful or poisonous, so the bright colour patterns of ladybirds are called warning colours. Warning colours are used as a defensive strategy by a wide variety of organisms. These species usually behave in a way which helps both to make them obvious to predators and to advertise their inedibility. Ladybirds often rest in exposed positions where they can easily be seen. They make little attempt to escape when disturbed, rather, they tend to 'play dead' by pulling their legs and antennae close into the body, and keeping still. Most species also exude a yellow fluid from pores in their leg joints. This is called 'reflex bleeding'. The secretion has a very bitter taste and an unpleasant smell. It runs along channels on the legs and forms yellow droplets at the edge of the pronotum and elytra (fig. 31).

Fig. 31. An eyed ladybird reflex bleeding.

That ladybirds are distasteful to many vertebrate predators has been confirmed by laboratory experiments. Frazer and Rothschild (1962) and Lane and Rothschild (1960) offered ladybirds to a variety of birds, mammals, reptiles, wasps and an amphibian. All rejected ladybirds. The toxicity of ladybirds depends on a number of different chemicals, including alkaloids, histamines and quinolenes (see Brakefield, 1985b). However, not all ladybirds are poisonous to all other animals, and some birds have been recorded eating ladybirds. Indeed some species of bird do seem to feed on ladybirds quite regularly. House martins are known to eat 2 spots, 7 spots, 10 spots, 11 spots and 14 spots. As these birds feed on the wing, catching flying insects, the ladybirds would have little chance of advertising their distastefulness before being devoured. The degree of protection afforded to ladybirds by their unpleasant properties is likely to vary with the species of ladybird, the ability of the predator to deal with the toxic ladybird chemicals, the predator's state of hunger, taste and scent perception, and its method of hunting.

Those species of ladybird which do not contain toxic chemicals, such as the larch ladybird, are not warningly coloured and do not reflex bleed. They obtain protection by being camouflaged. They have dull colours, lack bold patterns and tend to rest in sheltered or hidden positions.

It has recently been suggested that several species of ladybird employ both camouflage and warning colouration as defensive devices (Majerus, 1985). These are four species of Scots pine specialist: the eyed, striped, 18 spot, and cream-streaked ladybirds. Majerus noted that on the pines, the cream-streaked ladybird was very obvious from some distance away when it was moving about, or simply sunning itself on the pine needles and twigs. At such times the colour pattern seems to act as a warning advertisement. However, when resting, this species sits on pine shoots which it matches in colour and pattern to a very high degree. It is then extremely difficult to see. This ladybird is therefore warningly coloured when active or in an exposed position, and camouflaged when in its normal resting position. Similar observations have subsequently been made in respect of the eyed, striped and 18 spot ladybirds.

It has also been suggested that many of the warningly coloured species of ladybirds are Müllerian mimics (Rothschild, 1961; Muggleton, 1978; Brakefield, 1985b). When a number of species, each protected by some device such as a sting, a bite, or an unpleasant taste, resemble one another, they are said to exhibit Müllerian mimicry. This will evolve if predators need to learn which potential items of prey are inedible. If a number of inedible species look alike, then predators need learn only one pattern, and fewer of each prey species are killed than would be the case if each had a unique pattern which had to be learnt individually.

Brakefield (1985b and personal communication) hypothesised that most British ladybirds fall into four Müllerian mimicry complexes as indicated in table 8.

Table 8. *Brakefield's proposed Müllerian mimetic rings in ladybirds. (Based on Brakefield, 1985b.)*

Red or orange-red with black marks	Black with red marks	Yellow with black spots	Brown with yellow marks	Red-orange, pink or yellow, with black lattice pattern
7 spot	Pine	16 spot	Cream-spot	14 spot
5 spot	Kidney-spot	22 spot	Orange	Hieroglyphic
11 spot	Heather	Water	Cream-streaked	10 spot (f. *decempustulata*)
13 spot	2 spot (melanics)		18 spot	
Eyed	10 spot (f. *bimaculata*)			
Adonis'				
2 spot (non-melanic)				
10 spot (f. *decempunctata*)				

We feel that many of these groupings are rather artificial, and would question a number of the implied similarities, such as those in the two right-hand groups of table 8. The resemblances between some of these species are rather weak, and in such cases there is no experimental evidence to show that when predators have learnt one species they also avoid the others. In addition, this hypothesis produces a major problem in connection with variation in the 2 spot and 10 spot ladybirds. Brakefield suggests that the typical forms of these species are part of the black on red Müllerian complex, and that the melanic forms belong to the red on black complex. Were this true, one would expect melanic forms to be most common in areas in which there was an abundance of other red on black species such as the pine and kidney-spot ladybirds. Yet this is not the case. The frequencies of typical and melanic forms of the 10 spot show little variation from place to place. The frequencies of 2 spot forms do vary widely, but in areas where the pine ladybird is most common, the south-east of England and East Anglia, melanic 2 spots are rare, or absent. Although it does seem likely that the black on red colour patterns involve Müllerian mimicry, there are obvious

difficulties in explaining many of the other colour patterns
by this process. Furthermore, it is unlikely that predation
plays a significant part in maintaining variation in
warningly coloured and generally distasteful species, such
as the 2 spot, in which there is probably little predation by
predators, such as birds, which can discriminate between
the different forms.

6.3 The effect of selection in the 2 spot

The 2 spot ladybird is highly variable in its colour
pattern and the genetics of much of this variation has been
elucidated (see chapter 5). Why does this variation exist in
natural populations, and what selective forces are acting on
the different colour pattern forms so that form frequencies
vary between populations?

Most of the research on this problem has been
concerned with the differences between melanic and typical
forms. The early research established the geographic
distribution of the different forms, particularly the melanics,
throughout the range of the 2 spot. These studies, over
many years, have shown a high frequency of melanics only
from the climatic extremes of the species range, including
north-west and southern Europe as well as central Asia. In
Britain, high frequencies of melanic forms are found mainly
in urban populations in the north and west. But there are
exceptions to this pattern. For example, melanic forms have
been recorded at an appreciable frequency from some
populations in south-west London.

The low frequency of melanic forms in most 2 spot
populations suggests that they are at a considerable
selective disadvantage in most places. The nature of this
disadvantage has been the subject of much research. The
patterns of distribution suggest an association with climatic
factors. Lusis (1961), for example, suggested that melanic
forms heat and cool faster than non-melanic forms, and that
this reduces their survival under many conditions.
Timofeeff-Ressovsky (1940) found changes in the frequency
of forms between spring and autumn in Berlin. Melanic
ladybirds were commoner in the autumn than they were in
the spring. He suggested that in the spring and summer
melanic ladybirds warm up more quickly than typicals,
absorbing radiation faster than the red non-melanics.
Consequently they mate more often, thereby increasing their
reproductive output. This leads to the increase in melanic
frequencies observed during the summer. Among
overwintering ladybirds, mortality was greater in melanics

Map 1. The frequencies of melanic (black segments) and non-melanic (white segments) 2 spot ladybirds in Britain during the 1960s (after Creed, 1971). (Minimum sample size ten ladybirds.)

Map 2. The frequencies of melanic (black segments) and non-melanic (white segments) 2 spot ladybirds in Britain, 1985-1987. Data from the Cambridge Ladybird Survey. (Large circles: sample size more than 50 ladybirds; small circles: sample size 20-50 ladybirds.)

than in non-melanics. He attributed this to the greater fluctuations in temperature to which the melanics would be subjected; black surfaces absorb and emit radiation faster than red ones. The high winter mortality of the melanics would account for the drop in their frequency between autumn and spring.

Seasonal changes in form frequency have occasionally been reported from other places, including Britain, but the vast majority of studies have not revealed any consistent pattern. Nevertheless, other associations with climatic conditions are known. Scali and Creed (1975) found fewer melanics at higher altitudes in northern Italy, and attributed this to lower temperatures. In Britain, Muggleton and others (1975) found that the important environmental factor was not temperature itself, but the amount of sunshine. They suggested that because melanics absorb more radiation, they are more liable to overheat and desiccate in summer. This would explain the association between melanic forms and the urban areas of north-west Britain, because smoke pollution reduces levels of solar radiation.

Recent important observations have shown a decline in the frequency of melanic forms as aerial pollution has declined after anti-pollution legislation (maps 1 and 2). This strongly suggests a link between melanism in Britain and atmospheric pollution. It should be noted that the effect of being melanic during the spring and summer appears to be quite different in Berlin and Britain. In Berlin, because melanics absorb more radiation, their activity and reproductive output is greater than that of non-melanics. However, in many parts of Britain melanics are rare because, it is suggested, they absorb too much radiation. This is despite the fact that Britain has a cooler summer climate than Berlin. Such differences in interpretation highlight the difficulties encountered when attempting to interpret or explain 2 spot form frequency data. A correlation between high melanic frequency and high humidity has also been suggested. But it is clear that there is no uniform association between any one single climatic factor and form frequency throughout the range of the 2 spot (see Muggleton, 1978; Brakefield, 1985a).

Brakefield (1985b) suggests that melanic polymorphism in the 2 spot has evolved in response to selective factors associated with mimicry and bird

46

6 *Population and evolutionary biology*

polymorphism: the occurrence
of two or more distinctly
different forms of a species in
the same population

Map 3. The frequencies of
melanic (black segments),
chequered (halved segments)
and typical (white segments)
forms of the 10 spot ladybird in
Britain, 1985-1987. Data from
the Cambridge Ladybird Survey.
(Minimum sample size 40
ladybirds.)

predation. However, there is no evidence to support this
theory at present.

A more likely factor affecting the maintenance of
melanism, at least in Britain, involves the mating behaviour
of the ladybirds. Some female ladybirds from a number of
populations have been shown to prefer to mate with
melanic males rather than non-melanics (Majerus and
others, 1982a). This mating preference is itself under genetic
control, and not all females have the preference (Majerus
and others, 1982b, 1986). Those females which lack the
relevant gene mate at random. The reproductive advantage
gained by melanic males will certainly tend to increase the
frequency of melanics in the population unless other
selective factors are acting against melanics. The advantage
that melanics receive from this 'female choice' will be
greatest when melanics are rare, because when melanic
males are common the choosy females will be spread among
them more thinly than when they are rare. The females'
choosiness will therefore act to maintain the variation. As
melanics become rarer, the magnitude of the sexual selective
advantage will increase and so prevent the frequency of
melanics dropping further.

Despite all the work that has been done on variation
in the 2 spot, we are still far from understanding how it
evolved, or why it is maintained. Much research is still
needed and many questions remain unanswered. For
example, why is the frequency of the melanic form of the 10
spot relatively constant throughout the British Isles when
the frequency of melanic 2 spots varies so greatly from place
to place (see maps 2 and 3)? These species are closely
related and similar in many aspects of behaviour, ecology
and variation. Yet the melanic form of the 10 spot appears
in almost all British populations of the species, with
frequencies usually ranging from 5 to 20%, while melanic
forms of 2 spot are absent from many populations, but
comprise over 70% of others. Only by collecting form
frequency data over a long period of time, and by a close
and detailed comparison of the biologies and ecologies of
these two species, will the different factors influencing their
respective melanic polymorphisms be unravelled.

6.4 Evolutionary relationships

Figure 32 shows how species within the family
Coccinellidae are arranged into subfamilies, tribes and
genera. This diagram depicts hypotheses about
evolutionary relationships, because it is assumed that the

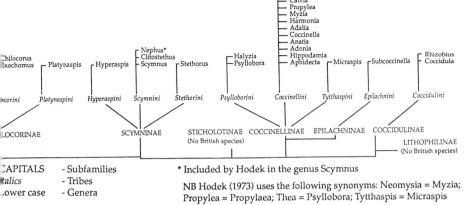

Fig. 32. The division of the family Coccinellidae into subfamilies, tribes and genera (British tribes and genera only) (adapted from Hodek,1973).

most similar species diverged most recently in evolutionary history.

To study evolutionary relationships, a number of characters need to be considered. They could involve almost any aspect of biology, be it behavioural, biochemical, anatomical or morphological. But characters used for studying relationships have to be chosen carefully. They must vary enough so that there are differences between species. It is also useful if the characters are easily studied. Mouthpart morphology is often used in the study of insect evolutionary patterns, but this character is of limited use in the ladybirds because the divergence that exists seems to reflect diet rather than evolutionary history. Carnivorous species have mouthparts quite different from those of the mildew feeders and the vegetarian 24 spot. The similarities in the mouthparts of the carnivorous species are probably examples of convergent evolution rather than a reflection of close evolutionary relationships; they resemble one another not because they have recently diverged but because they have the same function.

At the other extreme highly variable characters, such as colour patterns in ladybirds, are of little value in phylogenetic studies. New patterns emerge through simple genetic changes, so that a diverse range of colour patterns may occur in a single species. In addition, apparently similar colour patterns occur in distantly related species. For instance the pine ladybird resembles the *quadrimaculata* form of the 2 spot.

The characters most often used in phylogenetic studies of ladybirds are the genitalia. They are useful

phylogenetic: based on the closeness of evolutionary descent because they are highly variable through the group, each species having a unique apparatus, and because distinct trends are evident. One example of this is seen in the sipho, the part of the male genitalia inserted into the female during copulation. In primitive members of the tribe Coccinellini, the siphonal tube is short, thick and simple, and ends in a point. There are no examples of this type among the British fauna, but in the larch ladybird the sipho is short and pointed, with the only elaboration being an enlargement towards the middle and grooving along its length. In more advanced members of the group, the sipho is longer and more complex, often ending in a bulb, and the tube is often elaborately grooved and may bear flagella or other protuberances.

Phylogenetic study may involve a range of other characters. Many of these have not yet been used extensively in the Coccinellidae because they require live specimens and sophisticated techniques. The number, shape and size of chromosomes have been investigated to some extent (see chapter 9). Species of the tribe Chilocorini have chromosomes quite different from those of the Coccinellini. This is consistent with the idea, suggested by comparison of the morphology of the two tribes, that they diverged a very long time ago. Within the Coccinellini, the chromosome complement is rather uniform, most species having ten pairs. An exception is the genus *Anatis*, represented in Britain by the eyed ladybird. This species has fewer chromosomes than other members of the Coccinellini. There are also fundamental differences in the size and shape of the chromosomes, which set this genus apart from the other genera of the tribe. The evolutionary position of the genus *Anatis* is not clarified by comparative morphology. In some respects it approaches the genus *Calvia*, in others *Psyllobora*. However, its large size and type of colouration set it apart, and its relationships are still unclear.

The position is most likely to be clarified by molecular genetic analysis. In recent years it has become possible to sequence the order of nucleic acid bases in strands of the basic genetic material, DNA (deoxyribonucleic acid). This is the material of which genes are made and which passes from one generation to the next through evolutionary time. Differences in the order of nucleic acid bases along the DNA molecule can be used to determine the closeness of the relationship between a number of species. The DNA of very closely related species will differ little; that of more distantly related species will differ more. By comparing the sequences of nucleic acid

chromosome: small elongated bodies, consisting largely of DNA, in the nuclei of most cells, existing generally in a definite number of pairs for each species, and generally accepted to be the carriers of hereditary qualities

nucleic acids: long chain molecules of sugars, phosphate groups and bases which form the basic hereditary material of cells. There are five base types (adenine, thymine, cytosine, guanine and uracil) the sequence of which constitutes the genetic code and determines the products of genes bases in specific sections of DNA between representatives of all the genera in the tribe Coccinellini, the phylogenetic position of *Anatis* is likely to be discovered.

A similar approach involves gel electrophoresis, a technique which can be used to study variation in proteins encoded by genes (see chapter 9). Here again the sequences will be more similar in closely related species than in distantly related ones.

The sequencing of DNA or proteins requires expensive and sophisticated equipment, and for this reason it is unlikely to replace comparative morphology as the prime tool in classification. However, it is likely to be of considerable value in solving specific problems, such as the placing of *Anatis*, which have not been resolved by the more traditional approaches.

The different categories used to summarise the classification of species, namely the hierarchy of phyla, classes, orders, families, tribes and genera, are essentially based on arbitrary decisions regarding the rank to be assigned to each group. While it is hoped that the assignment of a species to a group is based on evidence, the assignment of a rank to each group often owes more to historical accident than to scientific insight. Named ranks are used for convenience to produce some order out of the chaos of the millions of different species which inhabit the earth today, and the millions more which have existed in the past but are now extinct. The one exception is the species. There have been many definitions of a species. One of the most sensible and commonly used is that a species consists of actually or potentially interbreeding groups of organisms, which are reproductively isolated from other such groups (Mayr, 1963). This means not only that individuals of a species must have the capacity to mate with one another, producing offspring which also have this capacity, but also that matings between individuals of different species should not produce viable and fertile offspring. The definition of species holds good for most sexually reproducing organisms. However, evolution is a dynamic process, and problems may arise with this definition in the case of groups which are undergoing, or have recently undergone, speciation. In such cases, the courtship and mating cues in different species may be similar enough to allow occasional hybrid matings. The occurrence of such hybrid matings in the wild usually suggests that the species involved have only recently diverged.

Studies of the occurrence and results of hybrid matings can be informative. Unconfirmed reports of hybrid

Fig. 33. Hybrid progeny from a cross between a chequered 10 spot and a weak *annulata* 2 spot, with markings similar to those of a 2 spot ladybird.

Fig. 34. Hybrid progeny from a cross between a chequered 10 spot and a weak *annulata* 2 spot, with markings similar to a 10 spot ladybird.

Fig. 35. Hybrid progeny from a cross between a chequered 10 spot and a weak *annulata* 2 spot, with unique markings.

Fig. 36. Hybrid progeny from a cross between a melanic 10 spot and a *quadrimaculata* 2 spot, with unique markings.

matings amongst British species of ladybird include the eyed with the striped ladybird, the 11 spot with the 7 spot, the 7 spot with the scarce 7 spot, the 10 spot with the 14 spot, and the 2 spot with the 10 spot. We ourselves have observed only two types of hybrid mating. One, involving a 5 spot female being mated by an 11 spot male, failed to produce any offspring. The other type, which we have observed on many occasions, is between 2 spot and 10 spot ladybirds (see Ireland and others, 1986). The number of eggs laid by females after such matings is relatively normal, but most of the eggs fail to hatch. Larvae which do hatch from hybrid eggs develop fairly normally and produce offspring, some of which are similar in appearance to 2 spots (fig. 33), others to 10 spots (fig. 34), and some of which have a unique pattern (figs. 35 and 36). All the progeny of our hybrid matings have been sterile. Examination of the hybrids has shown various reasons for their sterility. For example, of four sterile males examined, in one the testes were malformed, in a second there appeared to be no sperm formation, and in the other two the chromosomes behaved aberrantly during sperm formation so that chromosome breakages, and univalent (unpaired) chromosomes, were common.

The fact that the 2 and 10 spot ladybirds will hybridise and produce viable offspring supports the view that they are closely related, and suggests that their divergence is comparatively recent. However, the fact that the hybrid progeny are sterile confirms the view that they are distinct species.

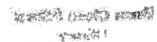

7 Ladybird distribution

7.1 Present or past residents in Britain

Despite their popularity, ladybirds have been little studied in Britain until recently. One major gap in our knowledge concerns the distribution of the different species in the UK. Attempts are currently being made to remedy this situation. An atlas of British ladybirds should soon be published, and a nationwide ladybird survey was launched in 1984 by workers at Cambridge University.

The atlas of British ladybirds is being produced by the Natural Environment Research Council's Biological Records Centre. Records are being compiled by Dr John Muggleton from the entomological literature, and from records sent in by interested entomologists over a number of years. The distribution maps are based on the 10km square system, whereby the country is split up into a grid of 10km x 10km squares (see chapter 9.1). Each ladybird species is recorded as present or absent in each particular 10km square.

Many of the records in the atlas are fairly old, so that the recorded presence of a particular species in a square means only that the species has been recorded in that square at some time; we may not know whether or not it still occurs there, particularly in the case of scarce species recorded only a few times each year, or rare species which may go several years without being recorded. For example, the 13 spot ladybird has not been recorded since 1950, and may now be extinct in Britain.

Not all of the 10km squares in the UK have been surveyed for ladybirds. In large areas of the UK, no ladybirds have been recorded. Is this because ladybirds do not occur in these areas, or simply because they have not been looked for? On the basis of a small study in 1986 the latter explanation seems more likely. One of the members of the Cambridge Ladybird Survey team spent four days in the north of Scotland looking for ladybirds in thirty 10km squares from which no ladybirds had previously been recorded. Despite spending only one hour searching each square, he found at least one species of ladybird in every square, and several squares yielded more than half a dozen species.

The common species of ladybird, which are often not recorded because they are not out of the ordinary, may be more generally distributed than records suggest. Apparent gaps in their distributions may be simply due to the fact that they have not been looked for in particular areas, or have been thought of as too common to be worthy of note.

It is hard to produce accurate distribution maps when the number of recorders varies from one area to another. Obviously, more records are made in areas where more people live. In general, the south-east of England is the most species-rich part of Britain for ladybirds. Both the species diversity and population density of ladybirds appear to drop away to the west and north. We have yet to discover how much this is a true reflection of ladybird distribution, and how much it is simply a manifestation of the number of ladybird recorders in different parts of Britain.

Because there are so many gaps in the distribution records of ladybirds, careful observation and collection will often be rewarded by the discovery of new records for particular 10km squares. Further details of the Coccinellidae Distribution Maps Scheme and of the Cambridge Ladybird Survey are given in chapter 9.

Generally the number of ladybird species declines as one goes north in the British Isles, but many species have a wide distribution, so even in the Highlands of Scotland nearly half the species may be found.

All the British ladybird species can be assigned to one of five distribution types: (a) widely distributed in a range of habitats; (b) widely distributed in specific habitats; (c) restricted distribution in a range of habitats; (d) restricted distribution in a specific habitat; (e) extremely rare species, possibly extinct or on the edge of extinction. The habitat preferences of many of the species have been dealt with in chapter 3.1. For example, the heather ladybird is a heather specialist, and is widespread on heathland in southern England. However, it is not found in the north of England, or in Scotland, so it is classed in category (d). Table 9 shows the distribution category of all the species. It also gives details of restrictions in distributions, and indicates the relative abundance of the different species.

Much can be learnt about the biology of particular species by the study of their geographic distribution. Some ladybirds, such as the 7 spot and cream-spot, seem to be able to cope with almost any climatic conditions found in the British Isles. On the other hand, the 11 spot, which is most often found on the coast, was at one time thought to require salt. However, Benham and Muggleton (1970) have shown that in south-east England it is also found inland on non-saline soils, and that its limitation to coastal areas further north seems to be due to climatic factors. Benham and Muggleton conclude that the most likely explanation of its distribution is that it is intolerant of wet conditions, but extremely tolerant of desiccation.

PLATE 1

1. *Coccinella 7-punctata*
   7 spot ladybird

2. *Coccinella magnifica*
   Scarce 7 spot ladybird

3. *Coccinella 5-punctata*
   5 spot ladybird

4. *Anatis ocellata*
   Eyed ladybird

5. *Anatis ocellata*
   Eyed ladybird

6. *Myzia oblongoguttata*
   Striped ladybird

7. *Harmonia 4-punctata*
   Cream-streaked ladybird

8. *Harmonia 4-punctata*
   Cream-streaked ladybird

PLATE 2

1. *Calvia 14-guttata*
   Cream-spot ladybird

2. *Myrrha 18-guttata*
   18 spot ladybird

3. *Hippodamia 13-punctata*
   13 spot ladybird

4. *Subcoccinella 24-punctata*
   24 spot ladybird

5. *Subcoccinella 24-punctata*
   24 spot ladybird

6. *Coccinella 11-punctata*
   11 spot ladybird

7. *Adalia 2-punctata* (f. *typica*)
   2 spot ladybird (typical)

8. *Adalia 2-punctata*
   (f. *quadrimaculata*)
   2 spot ladybird (melanic)

9. *Adonia variegata*
   Adonis' ladybird

10. *Adalia 10-punctata*
    (f. *decempunctata*)
    10 spot ladybird (typical)

11. *Adalia 10-punctata*
    (f. *decempustulata*)
    10 spot ladybird (chequered)

12. *Adalia 10-punctata*
    (f. *bimaculata*)
    10 spot ladybird (melanic)

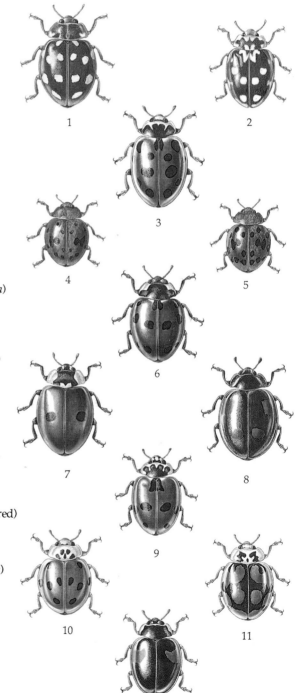

1

2

3

4

5

6

7

8

9

10

11

12

PLATE 3

1. *Propylea 14-punctata*
   14 spot ladybird

2. *Propylea 14-punctata*
   14 spot ladybird

3. *Psyllobora 22-punctata*
   22 spot ladybird

4. *Anisosticta 19-punctata*
   Water ladybird

5. *Micraspis 16-punctata*
   16 spot ladybird

6. *Halyzia 16-guttata*
   Orange ladybird

7. *Coccinella hieroglyphica* (f. *typica*)
   Hieroglyphic ladybird (typical)

8. *Coccinella hieroglyphica* (f. *areata*)
   Hieroglyphic ladybird (melanic)

9. *Aphidecta obliterata*
   Larch ladybird

10. *Chilocorus renipustulatus*
    Kidney-spot ladybird

11. *Chilocorus 2-pustulatus*
    Heather ladybird

12. *Exochomus 4-pustulatus*
    Pine ladybird

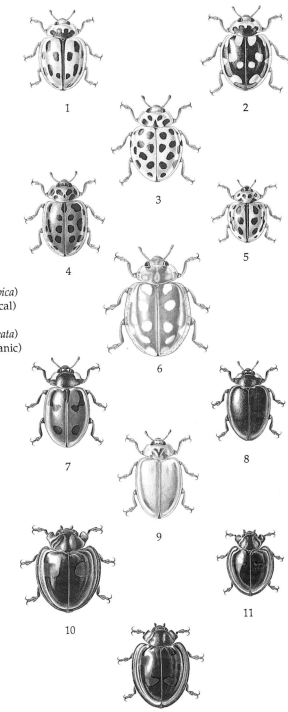

PLATE 4

Pigment development in the 2 spot ladybird (*Adalia 2-punctata*)

1-3: f. *typica*

4-9: f. *quadrimaculata*

Shown at various times
after emergence from the pupa

1. 30 minutes

2. 12 hours

3. 48 hours

4. 30 minutes

5. 1 hour

6. 3 hours

7. 12 hours

8. 24 hours

9. 48 hours

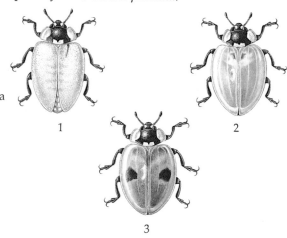

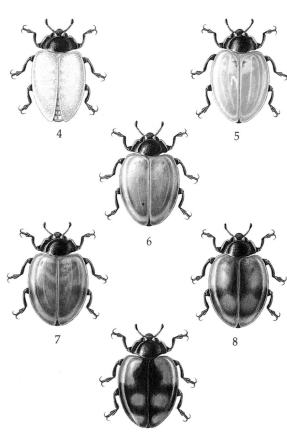

PLATE 5

Forms of the 2 spot ladybird

1. *sublunata*

2. *sexpustulata*

3. weak *annulata*

4. bar *annulata*

5. intermediate *annulata*

6. extreme *annulata*

7. *duodecempustulata*

8. new *duodecempustulata*

9. spotty

10. strong spotty

11. *sexpustulata* spotty

12. melanic *annulata*

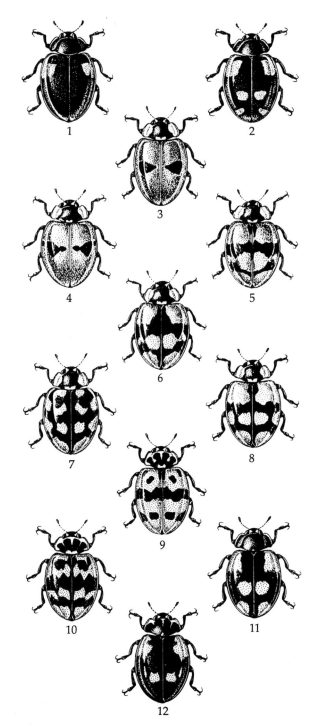

PLATE 6

Varieties of some British ladybirds

1. Eyed ladybird
   lacking cream rings

2. Eyed ladybird
   spots lacking black centres

3. 7 spot ladybird
   miniature spotted

4. Striped ladybird
   dark pronotal mark
   and additional stripes

5. Cream-streaked ladybird
   melanic

6. Larch ladybird
   boldly marked

7. Adonis' ladybird
   13 spotted

8. Adonis' ladybird
   5 spotted

9. 10 spot ladybird
   typical form with
   no elytra spots

10. 10 spot ladybird
    form *duodecempunctata*

11. 10 spot ladybird
    abnormally heavily marked
    chequered form

12. Hieroglyphic ladybird
    intermediate melanic

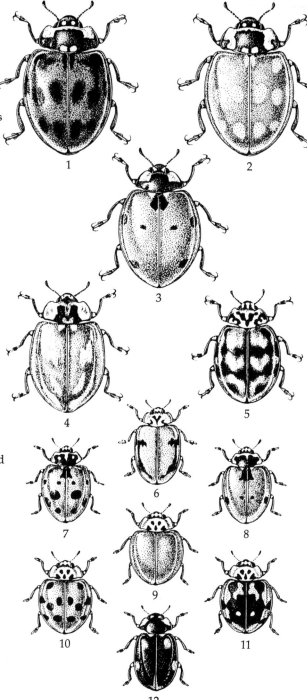

PLATE 7

1. *Rhizobius litura*

2. *Coccidula rufa*

3. *Coccidula scutellata*

4. *Hyperaspis pseudopustulata*

5. *Scymnus frontalis*

6. *Scymnus auritus*

7. *Platynaspis luteorubra*

8. *Vibidia 12-guttata*

9. *Exochomus nigromaculatus*

10. *Calvia 10-guttata*

11. *Procula douei*

12. *Cryptolaemus montrouzieri*

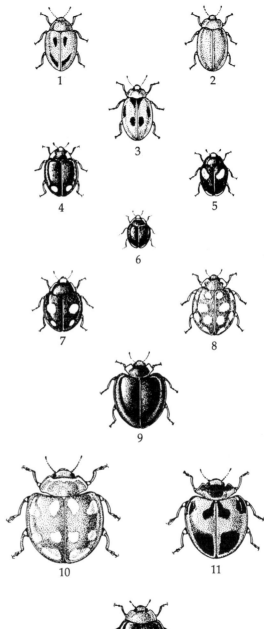

PLATE 8

Immature stages of ladybirds: eggs, larvae and pupae

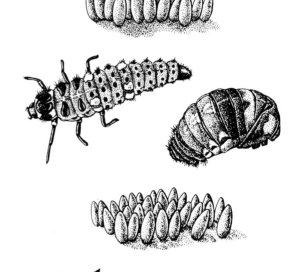

1. 7 spot ladybird

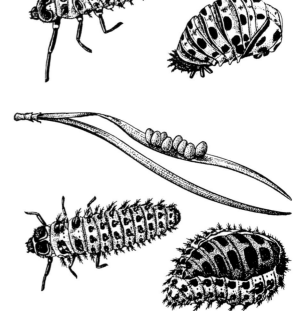

2. Eyed ladybird

3. Pine ladybird

Table 9. *General distribution status of British ladybirds*

Species	Distribution category and details
24 spot	c Common in southern and central England, and in Wales. Rarer in Scotland.
13 spot	e Probably extinct. No British records since 1950. Previously recorded mainly from eastern England. (See text and table 11.)
Adonis'	d Widespread but scarce in England and Wales.
Water	d Locally common in southern England.
Larch	b Common.
16 spot	c Common in southern England.
2 spot	a Abundant, scarce north of Inverness.
10 spot	a Common.
7 spot	a Abundant.
5 spot	e Very rare. Only recorded from four 10 km squares prior to 1987. Thought to be extinct in Britain until rediscovered in Wales and Scotland in 1987. (See text and table 12.)
11 spot	a Commonest near coasts, particularly the east, but also widely distributed inland in south-east England.
Scarce 7 spot	b Local and scarce.
Hieroglyphic	b Locally common.
Cream-streaked	d Widespread in southern and eastern England. Distribution spreading northwards, and westward.
Orange	b Local and scarce.
18 spot	b Widespread and locally common.
22 spot	a Common, but scarce in north England and Scotland.
Cream-spot	a Common.
14 spot	a Abundant, becoming less common northwards. Scarce north of Inverness.
Striped	b Common.
Eyed	b Common.
Kidney-spot	d Local in southern and central England and in Wales.
Heather	d Locally common in southern England and Wales.
Pine	b Abundant in southern England, becoming rarer further north. Scarce in Scotland.

Definition of distribution categories.

a - Widely distributed in a range of habitats.
b - Widely distributed in specific habitats.
c - Restricted distribution in a range of habitats.
d - Restricted distribution in specific habitats.
e - Extremely rare. Possibly extinct or on the edge of extinction.

The precise distributions of many species are determined by their habitat or host plant preferences. For example, although the larch ladybird is described as a widely distributed and common species, it is found almost exclusively on conifers, so the precise distribution is determined by the distribution of conifers. The same is true for many other species. This table should therefore be used in conjunction with table 3 (p.11) on habitat preferences.

The distributions of ladybirds are not static, but change from year to year due to changes in the environment, habitat destruction, and changes in the aphid populations. One of the most dramatic instances of changing geographical distribution concerns the cream-streaked ladybird. The first recorded British individual of this conifer specialist was found in west Suffolk in 1937. Since then it has spread south, west and northwards, so that it is now found over much of south-east and central England, and has also been recorded in south-east Scotland. The rate of spread from the initial colonisation can be seen by looking at the first years the species was recorded in different vice-counties (see table 10). This species seems to be well adapted to environmental conditions in Britain, and its spread through the British Isles will probably continue.

The cream-streaked ladybird is, however, almost certainly an exception; many of the other British species of ladybird are probably declining, both in numbers and in distribution. The main causes of such declines are habitat destruction, the use of fast-growing imported species of conifer in place of Scots pine as a timber plantation tree, and the use of chemical pesticides, many of which kill not only the target pests, such as aphids, but also the predators of the aphids. The extent of the decline in the ladybird fauna of Britain is difficult to assess. This is partly because of natural fluctuations in ladybird populations and partly because of the paucity of specific data on ladybird abundance and distribution until very recent times. However, the 13 spot

Table 10. *Cream-streaked ladybird – dates of first vice-county records*

West Suffolk, 1937	South Essex, 1976
East Suffolk, 1941	Cheshire, 1977
Berkshire, 1943	Oxfordshire, 1977
Cambridgeshire, 1948	West Kent, 1978
East Norfolk, 1953	East Kent, 1979
Surrey, 1956	Berwickshire, 1982 (first record
West Norfolk, 1957	from Scotland)
Huntingdonshire, 1957	North Hampshire, 1983
Buckinghamshire, 1950–1960	South Hampshire, 1984
East Gloucestershire, 1961	East Sussex, 1984
North Essex, 1970	West Sussex, 1985
Middlesex, 1972	Warwickshire, 1985
South-west Yorkshire, 1960–1973	Shropshire, 1986
South-east Yorkshire, 1960–1973	Dorset, 1986
North Lincolnshire, 1960–1973	Devon, 1987
Nottinghamshire, 1960–1973	Wiltshire, 1987
Staffordshire, 1976	

Records giving a range of dates indicate that the first record was made somewhere between the first and last date noted. We acknowledge the help of Dr J. Muggleton, of the Coccinellidae Distribution Mapping Scheme, in compiling this table.

ladybird is probably now extinct in Britain. It has only ever
been recorded from a handful of 10km squares, all on the
eastern side of Britain (see table 11). The most recent record
was around 1950. Another species which seemed to be in a
precarious position is the 5 spot ladybird. For some years it
was thought to have become extinct; until 1987 it had only
been recorded in two 10km squares in England, and two in
Scotland. The most recent of these records was in 1953 (see
table 12). However, the 5 spot was discovered in west Wales
in 1987. The ladybirds were found in some numbers on the
unstable river shingle on the banks of the Afon Tywi, the
Afon Ystwyth and the Afon Rheidol by recorders for the
Cambridge Ladybird Survey. Over 250 adults and larvae
were recorded from four different 10km squares in the
region during 1987. The species is probably quite widely, if
thinly, distributed in suitable habitats in west Wales. In 1987,
the 5 spot was also recorded from the Spey Valley in
Scotland near the place where it was recorded in 1953.
Again it was found on shingle. The species has probably
been present at suitable sites along the Spey Valley
throughout the intervening period.

Table 11. *All UK records of the 13 spot ladybird. (Data supplied by
Dr J. Muggleton on behalf of the Coccinellidae Distribution Mapping Scheme.)*

County	10 km square	Date
Northamptonshire	SP50	1819
Northumberland	NZ17,NZ18	pre-1889
Durham	NZ24	pre-1889
Greater London	TQ27	pre-1889
Kent	TQ65	pre-1913
East Sussex	TQ80	pre-1889, 1948
Kent	TQ87,TQ96	pre-1951
Kent	TR35	pre-1889
Essex	TM23	pre-1930

Table 12. *All UK records of the 5 spot ladybird. (Pre-1987 records supplied by
Dr J. Muggleton on behalf of the Coccinellidae Distribution Mapping Scheme.)*

County	10 km square	Date
Inverness-shire	NJ02	1912, 1935
Inverness-shire	NH90	1953
Devon	SX56	pre-1913
Dorset	SY29	circa 1941
Dyfed	SN57, SN67, SN68, SN73	1987
Inverness-shire	NJ13	1987

That a reasonably large and conspicuous ladybird, such as the 5 spot, should be rediscoverd, as the result of the increased interest in ladybirds engendered by the Cambridge Ladybird Survey, bears witness not only to the lack of ladybird records, but also to the potential discoveries which may await the observant ladybird spotter. Indeed, the 5 spot's rediscovery in 1987 gives hope that the 13 spot may yet be found again.

7.2 Immigrants, introductions and vagrants

Although one species of ladybird, the 13 spot, has probably become extinct in Britain this century, the arrival, establishment and subsequent spread of the cream-streaked ladybird means that we have also gained a species. Finding a new species of ladybird in Britain is obviously a rare event, but from time to time ladybirds previously unrecorded in Britain do turn up. The majority of such records are of vagrants probably imported into Britain accidentally by man. Many have been tropical species found near ports, and it is suspected that most arrived on cargo ships. The largest group of such vagrants is a series of species now housed in the Stevens Collection, in the British Museum (Natural History). They were collected between 1815 and 1845, mostly in the Bristol area.

There have been similar records of vagrants this century. For example, in the 1920s a specimen of a Jamaican species, *Procula douei* (pl. 7.11), was found in the New Forest, about ten miles from Southampton. But not all records can so easily be put down to accidental man-assisted importations. In 1927, a specimen of *Calvia 10-guttata* (pl. 7.10) was recorded at Killarney in Ireland. This large orange ladybird with pale spots had been recorded once previously in the west of England some time before 1861. This is a European species and the arrival on these islands of these vagrant individuals may not have been assisted by man. From time to time climatic conditions are such that insects are carried, more or less passively, for vast distances. Large amounts of sand and soil, sucked up from North Africa by the wind, have sometimes been deposited on northern Europe, including Britain. And on some of these occasions, beetles and other insects have been carried along by the wind with the sand and soil. Similarly, Britain is occasionally visited by species of insect from America, carried across the Atlantic by the prevailing south-westerly winds. The best known examples of this type are Monarch butterflies *(Danaus plexippus)*. It is therefore not impossible that natural forces may occasionally bring foreign species of ladybird to Britain. The records of *Calvia 10-guttata*, a central and southern

European species, may fall into this category. So may records
of two other species. One is *Vibidia 12-guttata* (pl. 7.8) which has
from time to time been included in the British list on the
strength of just a handful of records. This small orange
ladybird has white spots, and is a mildew feeder usually
found on deciduous trees. It is common in Europe and the
occasional British records are probably natural migrants.
The other is *Exochomus nigromaculatus* (pl. 7.9), a single
specimen of which was found in September 1967, near
Rossington Bridge on the outskirts of Doncaster (Skidmore,
1985). This species resembles the other British Chilocorini in
shape, but is immediately distinguished by the wholly black
elytra and broad yellow side margins of the pronotum.
Stephens (1831–2) recorded two British specimens, one
captured near Windsor in June 1816, the other taken near
Bristol.

The absence of any further records until 1967 has led
to the omission of the species from all lists of British
Coccinellidae apart from that of Donisthorpe (1939).
However, Skidmore (1985) makes a good case for reinstating
the species onto the British list, rather than considering the
1967 specimen purely as a casual import or immigrant. He
points out that the species, though most common south and
east of the Alps, does occur locally as far north as Denmark
and Sweden. Further, the 1967 specimen of *Exochomus
nigromaculatus* was found in its typical habitat of heather
heathland, and the species may occur in Britain as a very
rare and local resident.

Not all records of ladybirds which are considered to
be 'non-British' can be classed as accidental vagrants.
Because of their potential use in controlling aphids and
other plant pests, foreign ladybirds are, from time to time,
imported into Britain intentionally, so that feasibility studies
can be carried out on their usefulness. Although stringent
measures are usually taken to ensure that such imports do
not escape, some escapes undoubtedly do occur. The origin
of records of the ladybird *Cryptolaemus montrouzieri* (pl. 7.12)
are certainly accounted for in this way. This Australian
species has been used successfully in many parts of the
world to control mealy bugs or mealy aphids. They are bred
in this country for greenhouse use, and are available
commercially.

There are a considerable number of species of
ladybird which occur in continental Europe but are absent
from Britain. It is quite possible that some of these will one
day be transported across the English Channel or North Sea
and become established in Britain, much as the cream-
streaked ladybird has done over the last 60 years.

8 Identification of British ladybirds

Introduction to keys

This chapter consists of three keys, two for the identification of adult ladybirds, and one for their larvae. We do not encourage indiscriminate collecting or killing of ladybirds. Most ladybirds should be identifiable in the field, using the colour plates in this book, and the field key (key I), so that they can be released again where they are found*. Key I does not cover some unusual varieties or the smaller coccinellids which are not usually considered to be ladybirds. These may be identified using key II. Some of the characters used in key II will only be visible under a dissecting microscope, which means that the insects have to be collected. We have avoided using characters that make it necessary to kill the beetles, and we hope that whenever possible the insects are returned to the site of collection when a definite identification has been made.

Key III is designed to allow final instar ladybird larvae to be identified.

All these keys have been constructed using live material rather than dead museum specimens. Some keys to adult and larval keys already exist, and our choice of distinguishing characteristics owes a lot to these previous keys which we wish to acknowledge. They are Joy (1932), van Emden (1949), Pope (1953), Pope (1973), Hodek (1973), and Moon (1986).

Field key to adult British ladybirds

This key covers only the 24 species of coccinellid that we refer to as ladybirds (see table 1). It uses only characters easily seen in the field, and therefore it cannot cover every variety of ladybird in Britain. However, we think it covers all but a few rare variants, and should permit identification of over 99% of specimens.

---

* An identification card based on plates 1–3 of this book, and including details of habitat preferences, overwintering sites and hints to help with identification is available from Richmond Publishing Co.Ltd, P.O. Box 963 Slough, SL2 3RS.

We suggest that this key is used for field identification in conjunction with the colour plates (plates 1-3), which show the most usual forms of all the British ladybirds, and the black and white plates (plates 5 and 6), which illustrate some pattern varieties of the 2 spot and some of the commoner variants of other species. Specimens should first be compared with the plates. Then the field key should be used to check identifications made using the plates, or to name species in cases where comparisons with plates do not give a definite identification. If a specimen cannot be identified using this key, first check that it is a coccinellid using the basic diagnostic features of the group, particularly the leg segments (see key II). If it is a coccinellid, use key II. If an identification still cannot be made, we suggest that the specimen be referred to the British Museum (Natural History), or to one of the ladybird recording schemes (see chapter 9).

Most species of ladybird darken as they age (see chapter 5). This field key may not be much help with recently emerged adults which are still pale because the pigments have not been fully laid down.

A hand lens (x 10) and a ruler are useful for some parts of this key. The parts of a ladybird are named in II.1 and II.2 (page 66).

1 Upper surfaces covered in fine hairs (sometimes visible with the naked eye, but often only with a hand lens – take care). (Elytra and pronotum a uniform dirty or brownish red, with a variable number of black spots, often fused) (pl. 2.4 and 2.5)

24 spot ladybird (*Subcoccinella 24-punctata*)

– Upper surfaces not hairy   2

2 Ground colour of elytra not black   3
– Ground colour of elytra black   6

3 With markings on elytra   4
– Having no markings on elytra   11

4 Main elytra markings darker than the ground colour   5
– Main elytra markings paler than the ground colour   28

5 Ground colour of elytra bright orange-red or red   12
– Ground colour of elytra some other colour
   (e.g. yellow, pink, brown)   20

6   With pale (yellow, orange or red) markings at
    forward angle of elytra   7
–   Without pale markings at forward angle of elytra   9

7   Almost circular, with a definite lip around the edge of
    elytra. Two red marks on each elytron. (Forward angle
    mark curved (thicker at rear than at front) and just in
    from the marginal lip (I.1). Second mark round, just
    behind centre) (pl. 3.12)

I.1   Pine ladybird (*Exochomus 4-pustulatus*)
–   Body oval, with no lip around edge   8

8   Legs and underside of abdomen black. (Markings
    variable but usually with 1, 2, or 3 red or reddish orange
    spots on each elytron. If one spot, always at front angle
    touching the side margin (pl. 5.1); second spot (if
    present) round and central (pl. 2.8); third spot (if
    present) at tip) (pl. 5.2)

                                  2 spot ladybird (*Adalia 2-punctata*)

–   Legs brown, underside of abdomen orange or yellow;
    tip of abdomen usually brown or orange. (Forward
    angle mark curved, extending to margin, and widening
    towards margin (I.2). Markings red, orange or yellow)
I.2 (pl. 2.12)   10 spot ladybird (*Adalia 10-punctata*)

9   Body oval. (Completely black or with small tan
    markings at tip of abdomen and occasionally at each
    edge about half way along each elytron. Occasionally
    one or two small tan patches centrally) (pl. 3.8)

                            Hieroglyphic ladybird (*Coccinella hieroglyphica*)
–   Body round and well domed   10

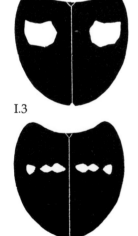

10 Head black (use a hand lens). Single large bright red or
I.3   orange spot centrally on each elytron (I.3). (Body almost
    circular with definite lip at edge) (pl. 3.10)

                          Kidney-spot ladybird (*Chilocorus renipustulatus*)
–   Head dark red (use a hand lens). Markings form a thin
    red band or row of two or three small spots across
    middle of elytron (I.4). (Body highly domed with lip
    around sides) (pl. 3.11)

                            Heather ladybird (*Chilocorus 2-pustulatus*)

I.4

I.5

11 Pronotum with four marks producing a distinctive M-shaped pattern (I.5). Elytra light brown, occasionally with pinkish tinge. (Body elongate) (pl. 3.9)

Larch ladybird (*Aphidecta obliterata*)

–   Pronotum with five dark marks. Elytra with ground colour of yellow, orange, orange-brown, red or red-brown. (Legs yellow, orange or brown) (pl. 6.9)

10 spot ladybird (*Adalia 10-punctata*)

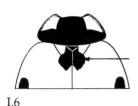

I.6

12 Scutellary spot present with two adjacent small white or off-white triangular patches on forward edge of the elytra (I.6)   13

–   Scutellary spot absent, or present but without flanking white patches   19

I.7

13 Elongate, about twice as long as broad. Pronotum with characteristic pattern (I.7). (Ground colour of pronotum usually yellowish. Usually with six black spots on each elytron in addition to the scutellary spot) (pl. 2.3)

13 spot ladybird (*Hippodamia 13-punctata*)

I.8

–   Less than twice as long as broad   14

14 Characteristic pronotum pattern (I.8). Number of spots on elytra very variable (see table 7) (pl. 2.9)

Adonis' ladybird (*Adonia variegata*)

–   Pronotal pattern not like this   15

15 Less than 5 mm long   16

–   5.5 mm or more in length   17

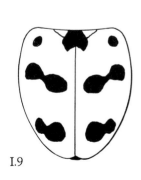

I.9

16 With five spots on each elytron in addition to scutellary spot (pl. 2.6). Occasionally hindmost pair of spots and/or middle pair of spots fused (I.9). Body somewhat elongate

11 spot ladybird (*Coccinella 11-punctata*)

–   With two spots on each elytron in addition to scutellary spot, the largest one central, the other behind the middle and near the edge of elytron. Body almost round (pl. 1.3)   5 spot ladybird (*Coccinella 5-punctata*)

I.10

17 Distinctive markings on pronotum (I.10). (Large, more than 7 mm long. Each elytron usually carries 7 or 8 black spots which are often, but not always, ringed with cream or yellow) (pl. 1.4 and 1.5)

Eyed ladybird (*Anatis ocellata*)

–   Pronotal pattern not like this   18

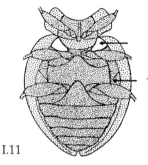

I.11

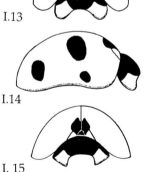

I.12

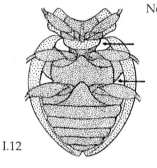

I.13

I.14

I. 15

I.16

18 Single small triangular white mark at each side on underside of thorax under middle pair of legs (I.11). (Usually three spots on each elytron in addition to scutellary spot. At least 5.5 mm long) (pl. 1.1)

7 spot ladybird (*Coccinella 7-punctata*)

–   Two small triangular white marks at each side on underside of thorax, one under each of the middle and hind pairs of legs (I.12). (Usually three or four spots on each elytron in addition to scutellary spot. At least 5.5 mm long) (pl. 1.2)

Scarce 7 spot ladybird (*Coccinella magnifica*)

Note. The scarce 7 spot is very similar to the much commoner 7 spot, and care needs to be taken when identifying it. The easiest way to distinguish the two species in the field is to place the ladybird upside-down in the palm of the hand. In a few moments it will begin to move its legs to try to right itself. In doing so it will expose the small white marks on the underside of the thorax. Both species have a pair of these marks under the middle pair of legs, but only the scarce 7 spot also has a pair under the hind legs. The marks are small and a hand lens may be needed to see them.

Although this is the most accurate diagnostic feature readily seen in the field, there are other differences which may be helpful. The scarce 7 spot has a more humped general shape. In particular the elytra drop almost vertically at the sides and back (I.13 and I.14), whereas in the 7 spot the elytra slope down to the margins more gently (I.15 and I.16). The front angles of the pronotum are rounded in the scarce 7 spot, somewhat pointed in the 7 spot. The central and hind spots are distinctly broader than they are long in the scarce 7 spot but not in the 7 spot, and are usually bolder than the corresponding spots in the 7 spot.

19 Legs black, underside of abdomen black. Markings variable (see pl. 5) but most commonly with a single black mark centrally on each elytron (pl. 2.7)

2 spot ladybird (*Adalia 2-punctata*)

–   Legs brown, underside of abdomen orange or yellow. Markings variable (see pl. 2.10, 2.11, 6.10 and 6.11). (There may be a number of small dark or black spots (usually an even number from 2 to 12) or a dark chequered pattern)

10 spot ladybird (*Adalia 10-punctata*)

I.17

I.18

I.19

I.20

20 2.5 mm long or less. (Ground colour off-white, pale grey or yellowish, with black markings, and a well defined, regular black line down join between elytra from scutellary spot to tip of elytra (I.17). Eight black spots on each elytron, the three at the side usually fused (I.18)) (pl. 3.5)

16 spot ladybird (*Micraspis 16-punctata*)

– More than 3 mm long 21

21 Between 3 and 5 mm long 22
– 5.5 mm long or more 27

22 Legs black. Scutellary spot flanked by white triangular patches on forward edge of the elytra (I.19). (Ground colour bronze or brown usually with three black spots – the foremost elongate – on each elytron) (pl. 3.7)

Hieroglyphic ladybird (*Coccinella hieroglyphica*)

– Legs not black 23

23 Pronotum with four brown or blackish marks producing a distinctive M-shaped pattern (I.20) (Scutellary spot absent. Body elongate, elytra light brown, occasionally with pinkish tinge) (pl. 6.6)

Larch ladybird (*Aphidecta obliterata*)

– Pronotal pattern not like this 24

24 Body elongate and rather flattened. Ground colour buff with yellowish or reddish tinge (sometimes pronounced). Nine black spots on each elytron in addition to scutellary spot. Six black spots, which may be fused, on pronotum (pl. 3.4)

Water ladybird (*Anisosticta 19-punctata*)

– Shape oval and somewhat domed 25

25 Femur of hind legs predominantly black. Underside of abdomen predominantly black. (Ground colour of elytra yellow, orange, orange-brown, or red-brown. Markings variable (see pl. 2.10, 2.11, 6.10 and 6.11) – there may be a number of small dark or black spots (usually an even number from 2 to 12) or a dark chequered pattern)

10 spot ladybird (*Adalia 10-punctata*)

– Femur of all legs yellow, orange or brown. Underside of abdomen orange or brown, particularly towards tip 26

26   Elytra bright yellow, with 11 evenly spaced discrete round black spots on each. Pronotum with five discrete black marks (pl. 3.3)

22 spot ladybird (*Psyllobora 22-punctata*)

–   Elytra yellow with distinctly squarish or rectangular black markings. There are 7 spots on each elytron but they are usually fused so that the number of spots cannot be counted. Black pronotum marks usually fused into single black splodge spreading forward from rear edge of pronotum. Underside mainly black. Legs orange (pl. 3.1 and 3.2)

14 spot ladybird (*Propylea 14-punctata*)

I.21

27   Between 5.5 and 7 mm long. Distinctive markings on pronotum (I.21). Ground colour yellow, tan or pinkish, often streaked with cream. (Elytra usually carry either 2 dark spots on the outer margin (pl. 1.7), or 8 dark spots (pl. 1.8) (occasionally fused) (pl. 6.5) spread across elytron)

Cream-streaked ladybird (*Harmonia 4-punctata*)

I.22

–   Large, 7 mm or more in length. Distinctive markings on pronotum (I.22). (Elytra deep reddish burgundy, each usually carrying 7 or 8 black spots which are often, but not always, ringed with cream or yellow) (pl. 1.4 and1.5)

Eyed ladybird (*Anatis ocellata*)

28   5 mm long or less   29
–   5.5 mm or more in length   32

I.23

29   Pattern on pronotum and at front end of elytra consistent and distinctive (I.23). (Ground colour of elytra and pronotum dark red-brown or maroon with off-white markings) (pl. 2.2)

18 spot ladybird (*Myrrha 18-guttata*)

–   Not like this   30

30   Ground colour maroon, purple or dark brown with a thick curved yellow, orange or red mark at front angle, extending to margin and widening towards sides (pl. 2.12)   10 spot ladybird (*Adalia 10-punctata*)

–   Markings not like this   31

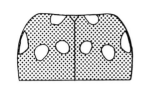

I.24

I.25

31 Ground colour brown or reddish brown with seven white, off-white, or cream spots on each elytron, three of which form an irregular band across the fore half of the elytron (I.24) (pl. 2.1)

Cream-spot ladybird (*Calvia 14-guttata*)

– Ground colour of elytra maroon, purple or dark brown with five bold cream, yellow or orange spots on each (pl. 2.11 and 6.11)   10 spot ladybird (*Adalia 10-punctata*)

32 Distinctive markings on pronotum (I.25). Large. (Elytra red, dark red or burgundy each with 7 or 8 rich cream spots [some of which may be centred with black]) (pl. 6.2)

Eyed ladybird (*Anatis ocellata*)

– Pronotal pattern not like this   33

33 Ground colour of elytra rich orange-red or chestnut, with rich cream or yellow stripes along the elytra (I.26). Large (pl. 1.6)   Striped ladybird (*Myzia oblongoguttata*)

– Ground colour orange with eight, or occasionally seven, white spots on each elytron (pl. 3.6)

Orange ladybird (*Halyzia 16-guttata*)

I.26

II Key to adult British Coccinellidae

This key covers all the British Coccinellidae, including the smaller species which are not generally regarded as ladybirds. These smaller species have not been covered in the main text of the book, but some details of their habitat preferences and distributions are given in table 13 (page 75). In constructing this key, our first consideration has been to choose characters which are absolutely diagnostic. When several distinguishing characters have been available, we have only used characters which are visible to the naked eye, or with a x 10 hand lens. It has not been possible to avoid more minute characters completely, and for some, differences may only be clearly visible under a dissecting microscope.

The key has been compiled using live material. Most previous keys have been based on dead museum specimens. Dead coccinellids tend to lose their natural colours fairly quickly. The paler colours, particularly the oranges and reds, become dull and often darken. Therefore, we have

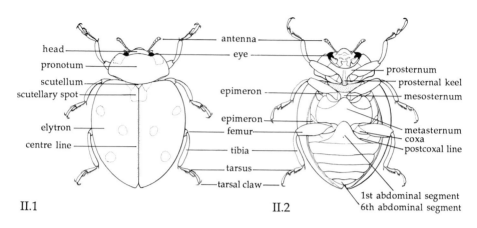

II.1

II.2

1st abdominal segment
6th abdominal segment

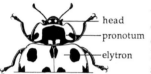

head
pronotum
elytron

II.3

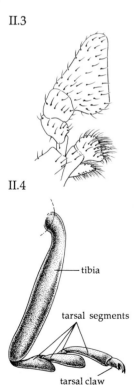

II.4

tibia

tarsal segments

tarsal claw

II.5

used colour sparingly as a diagnostic feature, except when a character is defined in terms of the positions of contrasting colours which will still be evident in dead specimens. We have sometimes had to use specialist names for anatomical structures. These are shown in figures II.1 and II.2.

The family Coccinellidae is diagnosed as follows. Small, less than 10mm long; convex, with an oblong oval, oval or hemispherical body shape. The head is retractable into the pronotum. The pronotum is broader than it is long and extends forwards at the margins (II.3). The eyes are large. The antennal sockets are close to the inner margin of the eyes and the antennae end in a three-segmented club. The mandibles (jaws) are large, and the maxillary palps (on the mouthparts behind the mandibles) are four-segmented with the end segment rather axe-shaped (II.4). The abdomen has from five to seven obvious segments, the first often having a humped central area. The legs are retractable into hollows beneath the body. The tarsi have four segments (three in the genus *Nephus*), but the third is small and often hidden within the deeply two-lobed second segment (II.5). Each tarsus bears two claws which may be simple, subdivided into two more or less equal pointed claws (II.6), or subdivided into a pointed claw and a blunt claw (II.7).

II.6

II.7

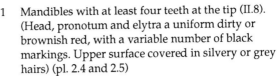

II.8

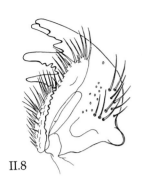

II.9

II.10

II.11

II.12

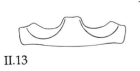

II.13

1   Mandibles with at least four teeth at the tip (II.8). (Head, pronotum and elytra a uniform dirty or brownish red, with a variable number of black markings. Upper surface covered in silvery or grey hairs) (pl. 2.4 and 2.5)

    24 spot ladybird (*Subcoccinella 24-punctata*)

–   Mandibles having just two teeth at the tip (II.9)   2

2   Lower front plate of head expanded sideways into a thin plate which covers the antennal sockets when viewed from in front (II.10)   3

–   Lower front plate of head not expanded sideways, antennal sockets visible when viewed from in front (II.11)   6

3   Body obviously hairy. Prominent prosternal keels present (see II.2). (Body oval. Colour black, usually with two red spots on each elytron, one central, the other near the rear tip) (pl. 7.7)   *Platynaspis luteorubra*

–   Body not hairy. Prosternal keels weak or absent   4

4   Postcoxal line which is on the first abdominal segment, seen from below, merges with the hind margin of the first abdominal segment (II.12). Tibia of front leg has a tooth on the outer margin   5

–   Postcoxal line on first abdominal segment, seen from below, does not merge with hind margin of the segment (II.13). Tibia of front leg without tooth on outer margin. (Shape almost circular with lip around edge of elytra. Ground colour black, with two red marks on each elytron, one at forward angle, the other just behind centre) (pl. 3.12)   Pine ladybird (*Exochomus 4-pustulatus*)

5   Head black (use a hand lens). Pronotum and elytra black with a single large red or orange spot centrally or just in front of middle of each elytron. 4.3 mm or more in length. (Body almost circular with a distinct lip at edge) (pl. 3.10)

    Kidney-spot ladybird (*Chilocorus renipustulatus*)

–   Head dark red (use a hand lens). Pronotum and elytra black with two or three small red spots, often fused into a band, across middle of each elytron. 4.1mm or less in length. (Body circular and highly domed with a lip around edge) (pl. 3.11)

    Heather ladybird (*Chilocorus 2-pustulatus*)

6   Antennae short, two-thirds or less as long as the width of the head (usually approximately equal to, or only slightly longer than, the diameter of the eyes). (Usually small, less than 3 mm long)   7

–   Antennae long, as long or longer than the width of the head. (Usually larger than above, more than 3 mm long)   20

7   Upper surface of elytra smooth. (Body oval, side margins of elytra and pronotum continuous (II.14). Colour black, with a yellow, orange or red spot at each side of the pronotum, and a red spot at the rear tip of each elytron.) (pl. 7.4)   *Hyperaspis pseudopustulata*

–   Upper surface of elytra hairy   8

II.14

8   Coxae of front legs large, prosternum greatly reduced both between coxae and in front of coxae with the narrow strip of prosternum in front of the coxae sloping down abruptly. (Colour usually black, with a curved yellowish mark on each elytron meeting on centre line to produce a horseshoe-shaped mark. More rarely, colour yellow with a black patch on elytra. Less than 1.5 mm in length)   *Clitostethus arcuatus*

–   Coxae of front legs normal, prosternum between coxae normal, and prosternum in front of coxae not narrowed and not markedly down-sloping   9

9   Prosternal keels present. Tarsi 4-segmented (II.15)   10
–   Prosternal keels absent. Tarsi 3-segmented (II.16)   17

II.15

II.16

10 Postcoxal line incomplete, but reaches to the rear margin of first abdominal segment (seen from below) before curving forward again (II.17)   11

–   Postcoxal line complete, curving out and back, but only reaching between halfway and two-thirds of the way back across the first abdominal segment before curving forward to join the front margin again (II.18)   14

II.17

11 Completely black, including legs, antennae, and all mouthparts. Pits on elytra all of one size
                                                            Scymnus nigrinus
–   Antennae, tibiae and maxillary palps pale. Pits on elytra of two sizes   12

II.18

12 Each elytron sports a large pale red patch forward of the middle (pl.7.5)   *Scymnus frontalis*
–   Elytra completely black, or black with just a pale outer margin   13

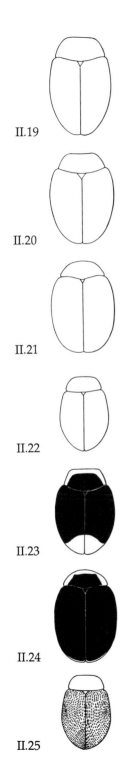

II.19

II.20

II.21

II.22

II.23

II.24

II.25

13 2.4 mm or more in length. Shape somewhat elongate (II.19). Metasternum with a groove along centre line
Scymnus schmidti

– 2.3 mm or less in length. Shape oval (II.20). Metasternum lacking a groove along centre line
Scymnus femoralis

14 Front area of side margins of elytra convexly curved (II.21). Elytra black except for pale area at the rear tip which may be a broad patch or a narrow margin. Legs with the tibiae yellow. Front margin of pronotum usually paler than the rest of the pronotum   15

– Front area of side margins of elytra almost straight (II.22). Elytra red-brown, or chestnut brown becoming darker towards the centre line and side margins. Tibiae dark brown or black. Pronotum of uniform colour   16

15 Elytra with a large patch of yellow or orange-brown at rear tip (II.23). Prosternal keels converge towards the front   *Scymnus haemorrhoidalis*

– Elytra black except for a very thin pale border around the margin of the rear part (II.24). Prosternal keels do not converge towards the front and are well separated at the front margin of the prosternum (pl. 7.6)
Scymnus auritus

16 1.7 mm or less in length. Pits on elytra all of about the same size, intervals between pits approximately one pit diameter, and plain. Hairs lie rather flat and lie in a distinct direction (II.25). (Elytra red or red-brown centrally, darkening to black at centre line and side margins.)   *Scymnus limbatus*

– 1.9 mm or more in length. Pits on elytra of two distinct sizes and separated by less than the pit diameter; interval between pits is wrinkled. Hairs more or less erect and do not produce a directional pattern. (Elytra red or red-brown usually with a dark brown mark behind the scutellum)   *Scymnus suturalis*

17 Body almost hemispherical. (Black except for antennae, tibiae, tarsi and labrum (upper 'lip' of mouthparts) which are usually yellow or brown)
Stethorus punctillum

– Body longer than wide   18

18 Pronotum with few minute pits; surface of pronotum between pits minutely wrinkled. Elytra black and unmarked except for a very narrow yellow or orange border at the rear end. Occasionally there is a faint dull reddish patch on each elytron towards the rear tip; it never extends forwards as far as the middle
Nephus bisignatus

–   Pronotum with many obvious pits, and smooth between. Elytra black with obvious yellow, orange or red patches which extend to front half of elytra   19

II.26

19 Each elytron with two well defined yellow spots, one forward and one behind the middle (II.26). Pits on elytra shallow   *Nephus quadrimaculatus*

–   Each elytron with a single large orange patch extending from close to the rear tip to near the scutellum (II.27). The edges of this patch are often indistinct. Pits on elytra deep   *Nephus redtenbacheri*

II.27

20 Upper surfaces hairy   21
–   Upper surfaces not hairy   23

21 Pronotum broadest at rear margin, with a groove running across at the base. Body oval (II.28). Pits on elytra scattered randomly. Tarsal claws with a single point and a secondary blunt tooth. (Ground colour reddish or ochreous with a dark streak running forwards and to the sides from close to the rear tip of the centre line. A dark patch behind the scutellum also present. Hindwings often reduced) (pl. 7.1)
Rhizobius litura

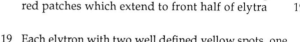

–   Pronotum broadest in front of middle, lacks a groove across it at the base. Body rather elongate, the sides almost parallel (II.29). Some pits on elytra arranged in longitudinal rows, others scattered more randomly. Tarsal claws double-pointed   22

II.28

22 Elytra reddish-brown and unmarked or having at most a small dark spot at each shoulder (pl. 7.2)
Coccidula rufa

–   Elytra reddish-brown with a triangular black scutellary spot and two black spots on each elytron, one at the side, at or slightly in front of the middle, the other close to the centre line about half to two-thirds of the way back (pl. 7.3)   *Coccidula scutellata*

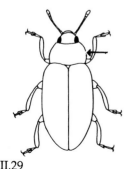

II.29

23 Body elongate. Front half of outer margins of elytra straight or with a slight concave curve. Pronotum broadest at, or in front of, middle. Central projection of the first abdominal segment (seen from below) is bordered by a strongly raised ridge   24

– Body outline oval or rounded. Outer margins of elytra entirely convex. Pronotum broadest behind middle. Central projection of the first abdominal segment lacks a bordering raised ridge   25

II.30

24 4.1 mm or less in length. Mesosternum has an abrupt squared-off end between the mid-coxae. Tarsal claws untoothed (II.30). (Body flattened in appearance. Ground colour buff with yellowish or reddish tinge. Nine black spots on each elytron and a shared scutellary spot. Six black spots on pronotum which may be fused) (pl. 3.4)   Water ladybird (*Anisosticta 19-punctata*)

– More than 4.5 mm in length. Mesosternum tapers to a point between mid-coxae. Tarsal claws divided into two teeth of unequal size by a deep cleft (II.31). Pronotum with characteristic pattern (II.32). (Ground colour of pronotum usually yellowish) (pl. 2.3)

    13 spot ladybird (*Hippodamia 13-punctata*)

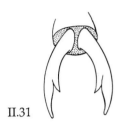

II.31

II.32

25 Tarsal claws divided into two pointed teeth by a deep cleft (II.33)   26

– Tarsal claws with one pointed tooth divided from a second blunt, squared-off tooth (II.34)   27

II.33

II.34

26 Less than 5.5 mm long. Segments of antennal club broader than they are long. Characteristic pronotal pattern (II.35). (Ground colour red with variable number of black spots, including a scutellary spot flanked by two triangular white patches) (pl. 2.9)

    Adonis' ladybird (*Adonia variegata*)

– More than 6 mm long. Segments of antennal club longer than broad. Sides of pronotum off white with chestnut, brown, or black M mark filled with chestnut or orange-red. (Ground colour rich orange-red or chestnut, very rarely chocolate brown, with rich cream or yellow stripes along the elytra (II.36)) (pl. 1.6)

    Striped ladybird (*Myzia oblongoguttata*)

II.35

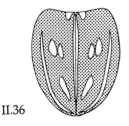

II.36

27 Scutellum very small and virtually hidden under the base of the elytra when these are closed. 2.5 mm long or less. (Ground colour off-white, pale grey, or yellowish, with black markings consisting of a black centre line

(II.37), and eight spots on each elytron, the outer three usually fused (II.38)) (pl. 3.5)

16 spot ladybird (*Micraspis 16-punctata*)

– Scutellum triangular, of normal size and visible when elytra are closed 28

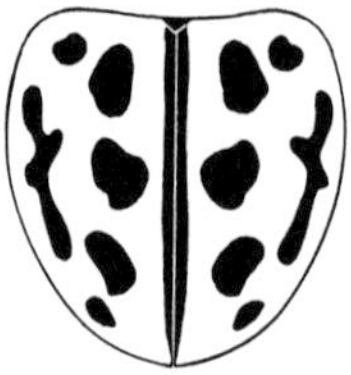

II.37

28 Segments of antennal club compact, as broad as, or broader than, long and with flat apical margins (II.39) 29

– Segments of antennal club appear looser, longer than broad, and/or with the apical margin bowed internally (II.40) 36

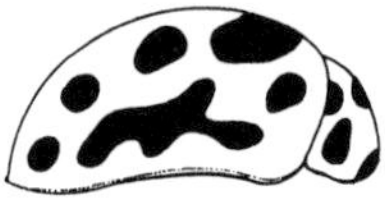

II.38

29 Prosternal keels absent 30

– Prosternal keels present 32

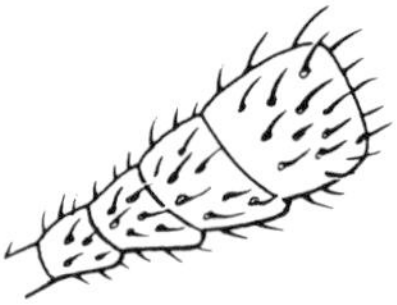

II.39

30 More than 5.5 mm long. Postcoxal line on first abdominal segment merges with hind margin (II.41). Elytra with fine filigree sculpturing between pits. (Distinctive markings on pronotum (II.42). Ground colour yellow, tan or pinkish, often streaked with cream. Each elytron usually carries either 2 dark spots on outer margin (pl. 1.7), or 8 dark spots) (pl. 1.8)

Cream-streaked ladybird (*Harmonia 4-punctata*)

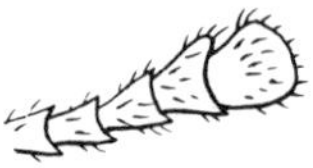

II.40

– Length 5 mm or less. Postcoxal lines on first abdominal segment incomplete, reaching only two-thirds of the way to the hind margin and then curving forward (II.43). Elytra smooth between pits 31

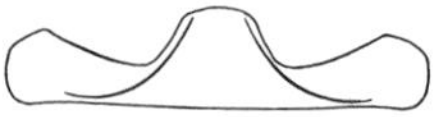

II.41

31 **Meso**sternal epimera black. Front margin of mesosternum between coxae not notched. Legs black. (Body oval. Ground colour usually red with black markings or reverse, with very variable patterns) (see chapter 5, pl. 2.7, 2.8 and 5)

2 spot ladybird (*Adalia 2-punctata*)

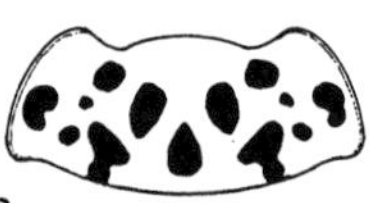

II.42

– **Meso**sternal epimera yellow, orange or brown. Front margin of mesosternum notched. Legs generally yellow, orange or brown. (Body almost round. Colour of elytra and markings extremely variable) (see chapter 5, pl. 2.10, 2.11, 2.12, 6.9, 6.10 and 6.11)

10 spot ladybird (*Adalia 10-punctata*)

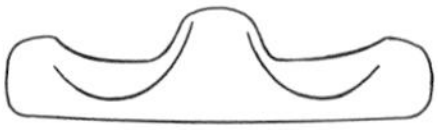

II.43

32 **Meso**sternal epimera black. Scutellary spot elongate. Elytra bronze or brown with black markings or black with tan markings, or almost completely black (pl. 3.7, 3.8 and 6.12)

Hieroglyphic ladybird (*Coccinella hieroglyphica*)

– **Meso**sternal epimera white. Scutellary spot round or broader than long. Elytra red with black spots 33

33 **Meta**sternal epimera white. Front angles of pronotum somewhat rounded (II.44). Elytra obviously covered with network sculpturing between pits (pl. 1.2)
Scarce 7 spot ladybird (*Coccinella magnifica*)

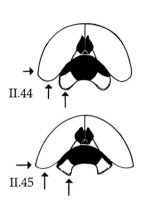

II.44

– **Meta**sternal epimera black. Front angles of pronotum somewhat pointed (II.45). Elytral surface smooth or almost smooth between pits 34

II.45

34 Prosternal keels diverging to the front. Body rather rounded (ratio of length to width not more than 5:4). Pits on head between the eyes separated by their own diameter or less 35

– Prosternal keels parallel. Body elongate (ratio length to width 6:4 or more). Pits on head between eyes separated by much more than their own diameter. (Elytra with five spots on each and shared scutellary spot. Spots may be fused) (pl. 2.6)
11 spot ladybird (*Coccinella 11-punctata*)

35 5.5mm or more in length. Body oval. Prosternum black with small white patches in front outer angles, these being much less extensive than the white marks on the pronotum. (Elytra usually with three black spots on each and a shared scutellary spot) (pl. 1.1)
7 spot ladybird (*Coccinella 7-punctata*)

– 5mm or less in length. Body round. Prosternum black with large white patches in front outer angles, these being as extensive as white pronotal marks. (Elytra usually with two black spots on each and a shared scutellary spot) (pl. 1.3)
5 spot ladybird (*Coccinella 5-punctata*)

II.46

36 More than 7 mm long. Distinctive pronotal pattern (II.46). (Elytra usually deep reddish burgundy but somewhat variable, most commonly with 7 or 8 black spots on each, often but not always ringed with cream. Occasionally one or more of the black spots is absent leaving a cream spot) (pl. 1.4 and 1.5)
Eyed ladybird (*Anatis ocellata*)

– Less than 6.5 mm long. Pronotal pattern not as above 37

II.47

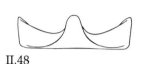

II.48

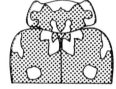

II.49

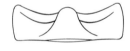

II.50

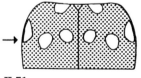

II.51

37 Body elongate. Pronotum with groove across near hind margin. Pronotum with distinctive M-shaped marking (II.47). (Elytra light brown, occasionally with pinkish tinge, and unmarked, or with fine dark longitudinal streak) (pl. 3.9 and 6.6)

Larch ladybird (*Aphidecta obliterata*)

–   Body round or oval. Pronotum without cross groove. Pronotum without M-shaped mark   38

38 Having pale markings on a dark but not black ground colour   39

–   Either having black marks on a pale (usually yellow) ground colour, or pale (usually yellow) marks on a black ground colour   41

39 Mesosternum with front margin straight. Ground colour yellow or orange. (Elytra have 7 or 8 white or pale lemon yellow spots on each) (pl. 3.6)

Orange ladybird (*Halyzia 16-guttata*)

–   Front margin of mesosternum slightly or strongly notched. Ground colour maroon or brown   40

40 Front margin of mesosternum slightly notched. First abdominal segment as in II.48. Distinctive pattern of off-white spots on pronotum at front of elytra (II.49)
      (pl. 2.2)   18 spot ladybird (*Myrrha 18-guttata*)

–   Front margin of mesosternum strongly notched. First abdominal segment as in II.50. Seven off-white or cream spots on each elytron, three of which form a band across the fore half of the elytron (II.51) (pl. 2.1)

Cream-spot ladybird (*Calvia 14-guttata*)

41 Prosternal keels absent. (Ground colour of pronotum and elytra bright yellow, with five separate black spots on pronotum and 11 rather round spots on each elytron) (pl. 3.3)   22 spot ladybird (*Psyllobora 22-punctata*)

–   Prosternal keels present. (Ground colour yellow with distinctly squarish or rectangular black markings, or the reverse. Black markings on the pronotum usually fused into a single black area spreading forward from rear edge of pronotum. Underside mainly black) (pl. 3.1 and 3.2)   14 spot ladybird (*Propylea 14-punctata*)

Table 13. *Habitat preferences and geographic distributions of British coccinellids, not generally considered to be ladybirds*

Species	Preferred habitat	Distribution
Platynaspis luteorubra	Low growing vegetation, grasslands. Probably lives in association with ants such as *Lasius niger*. †	Local and rare in southern England. ††
Hyperaspis pseudopustulata	Deciduous woodland, orchards. Often found in moss on or below trees.	Widely distributed and often common.
Clitostethus arcuatus**	Deciduous and coniferous woodland.	Local and rare in south and central England. ††
Scymnus nigrinus**	Conifer woodland, particularly Scots pine.	Common in south and central England. Scarce elsewhere. Absent from Wales. ††
Scymnus frontalis**	Low growing vegetation, usually in dry habitats or coastal dunes.	South-east England, East Anglia and on coasts from Merseyside south around to East Anglia. ††
Scymnus schmidti*	Low growing vegetation, usually in dry situations.	Disjunct distribution. Widespread but local in south-east England. Also recorded from some western coasts.
Scymnus femoralis	Low growing vegetation, on chalk or sandy soils. †	Not uncommon in south-east England. Only a few records from elsewhere.
Scymnus haemorrhoidalis*	Low growing vegetation and shrubs. Usually in damp areas.	Widespread in south-east England, rarer to the north and west. Not recorded from Wales or Scotland. ††
Scymnus auritus	Oak woodland.	Widespread throughout England and east Wales. Very rare in Scotland.
Scymnus limbatus*	On willows, sallows and poplars.†	Local and scarce. Confined to south-east England and East Anglia. ††
Scymnus suturalis*	Conifer woodland, particularly Scots pine.	Widespread and common in England and Scotland. Uncommon in Wales.
Stethorus punctillum	Deciduous woodlands, orchards and hedgerows (feeds on *Phyllacotes* mites).	Widespread in south and central England. Locally common or abundant. ††
Nephus bisignatus*	Low growing vegetation. †	Very rare. Only three known British specimens, all from the south-east coast. May not be resident. ††
Nephus quadrimaculatus**	Conifer woodland, particularly Scots pine. Sometimes found on ivy.†	Very rare. Confined to Kent and East Anglia. ††
Nephus redtenbacheri*	Grassland and low growing vegetation.	Widespread and locally common throughout Britain.
Rhizobius litura	Grassland, meadowland and low growing vegetation. Often on nettles.	Widespread and often common.
Coccidula rufa	On reeds (*Phragmites*), rushes (*Juncus*), and reed mace (*Typha*) in wetlands. Occasionally grassland.	Widespread and locally common throughout Britain.
Coccidula scutellata	On reeds (*Phragmites*), rushes (*Juncus*), and reed mace (*Typha*) in wetlands.	Widespread and locally common in south and central England. Scarce in Wales.

* Early stages unknown.
** No notes on early stages from Britain.
† Habitat preferences based on few records and probably incomplete.
†† British distribution based on few records and probably incomplete.

III Field key to the larvae of British ladybirds

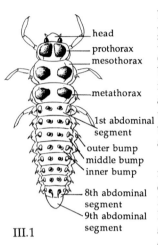

head
prothorax
mesothorax

metathorax

1st abdominal
segment
outer bump
middle bump
inner bump
8th abdominal
segment
9th abdominal
segment

III.1

This key is designed to allow fourth instar larvae of British ladybirds to be identified in the field. With a little practice it is easy to distinguish a ladybird larva from the larvae of other beetles, at least in its later instars. It has an elongate slender body. The body is arched on top and flat below; it is not cylindrical. It is not glossy; the upper surface is covered in small distinct bumps giving a rough appearance. Older larvae are often brightly coloured with white, yellow, orange or black spots. Ladybird larvae are usually found on plants, near their prey or food. Often adults and pupae will be found near the larvae.

Although this key is based on fourth instar larvae, many younger larvae should key out. There are reasonably consistent changes in larval morphology between instars. First and second instar larvae are not brightly coloured and lack distinct bumps on the thoracic and abdominal segments. Third and fourth instar larvae are brightly coloured and have dark plates on the thorax, with distinct bumps on the thorax and abdomen. Although many third and some second instar larvae may key out correctly, those who wish to identify younger larvae may have to refer to more detailed and comprehensive keys to coccinellid larvae, such as those by van Emden (1949) or Hodek (1973).

The formal separation of the larvae of many beetle families depends on the structure and shape of the head, antennae, mouthparts, legs and abdominal appendages. If from the general appearance of a larva it is not obvious whether it is a ladybird larva or not, van Emden's *Key to the British Families of Beetle Larvae, for Ready Identification* (1942) may be consulted, although a fair knowledge of larval morphology is necessary to use the key.

The diagnostic features of larvae of the Coccinellidae are as follows. Body elongate and slender, arched above and flat below. Head hard, dark and shiny, rather squarish with rounded corners. The head capsule has well developed fault lines (III.7, page 78). The antennae have three segments, the first being short, the second longer and thinner with a spine, and the third small. Mouthparts: mandibles (jaws) very dark and triangular, usually with one or two teeth at the tip (four or more in the 24 spot); the maxillary palps three-segmented; labial palps with one or two segments. The legs are elongate. The femur and tibiotarsus are cylindrical.

This key is based on characters which can be seen with the eye or with a x 10 hand lens. Most keys to the larvae of ladybirds rely on minute characters that require

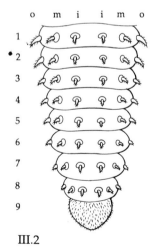

o   m   i   i   m   o

1
• 2
3
4
5
6
7
8
9

III.2

II.3

II.4

III.5

III.6

dissection and microscopic examination. This key attempts to avoid the need for such techniques. The larvae of all 24 species of British ladybird listed in table 1 should be identifiable using the obvious characters used in this key, with the exception of one pair of species. The more detailed characters which need to be examined to separate these two species are given in square brackets in the key.

This key does not cover the larvae of the smaller coccinellids which are not generally considered to be ladybirds. If you find a larva which appears to be a coccinellid but does not key out, consult van Emden (1949) or Hodek (1973). Note that these other species are smallish, and their larvae are also small. Doubt about the identification of any larva can be resolved by rearing it to the adult stage to check the identification.

Fig. III.1 shows the various parts of a ladybird larva which are mentioned in the key.

Each of the first eight abdominal segments bears a row of six structures (bumps, warts, spines), three on each side of the central line (III.2). In the key, these structures are referred to by giving the segment on which the structure is situated (e.g. Ab 4 means fourth abdominal segment) with a letter (o for outer, m for middle and i for inner) to indicate which of the three structures to one side of the central line is being discussed.

1   Meso- and meta-thorax each with two hair-bearing bumps low on the side (III.3)   2

–   Meso- and meta-thorax each with one hair-bearing bump low on the side (III.4)   5

2   Body with warts on top or sides which are not higher than they are broad at the base. (Body pale brown-grey with conspicuous black hairs)

        16 spot ladybird (*Micraspis 16-punctata*)

–   Body with spines on top or sides which are higher than they are broad at the base   3

3   Spines with distinct short branches each bearing a single hair (III.5). Ab 1 o and m paler than Ab 1 i

        Pine ladybird (*Exochomus 4-pustulatus*)

–   Spines not branched, but with hairs (III.6)   4

4   Ab 1 i, m and o dark

Kidney-spot ladybird (*Chilocorus renipustulatus*)

–   Ab 1 i, m and o pale. (Ab 1 i with black central dot. Ground colour of first abdominal segment off-white)

Heather ladybird (*Chilocorus 2-pustulatus*)

III.7

5   Fault line on head capsule shaped like an inverted Y (III.7). (Spines branched, pronotum bears a single row of four spines along front margin. Ground colour pale greenish grey)

24 spot ladybird (*Subcoccinella 24-punctata*)

–   Fault line on head capsule shaped like an inverted pot (III.8)   6

III.8

6   Final (ninth) abdominal segment ending with a distinctly pointed protuberance (III.9)   7

–   Final (ninth) abdominal segment lacking a pointed protuberance at the end, and usually rounded (III.10)   8

III.9

7   Upper side of abdominal segments has branched spines bearing hairs. (Hind margin of pronotum bears a row of eight hairy spines)

Cream-spot ladybird (*Calvia 14-guttata*)

–   Upper side of abdominal segments bears hairy warts (not spines)   14 spot ladybird (*Propylea 14-punctata*)

III.10

8   Ground colour of abdomen yellow   9

–   Ground colour of abdomen light grey, blue-grey, grey, brown or black   10

9   Head dark brown. Ab 1 m yellow. Legs shorter than head width   22 spot ladybird (*Psyllobora 22-punctata*)

–   Head pale yellow with darker markings. Ab 1 m black. Legs longer than head width

Orange ladybird (*Halyzia 16-guttata*)

10   Warts or spines on abdomen all of similar colour. (Ground colour brownish)

Water ladybird (*Anisosticta 19-punctata*)

–   Warts or spines on abdomen of several distinctly different colours   11

11   Ab 1–4 m and Ab 4 i orange or yellow. (Ground colour dark grey. Spines three pointed with black tips)

Cream-streaked ladybird (*Harmonia 4-punctata*)

–   Ab 2–3 m dark   12

12 Ab 2 o pale   13
 – Ab 2 o dark   14

13 Ab 3–4 o dark. (Pronotum with a row of six obvious
    spines along hind margin)
                              Eyed ladybird (*Anatis ocellata*)
 – Ab 3–4 o pale   Larch ladybird (*Aphidecta obliterata*)
                      or 18 spot ladybird (*Myrrha 18-guttata*)
    [Larch ladybird:- ground colour usually pale greyish
    yellow on upper surface. Legs uniformly coloured.
    Many hairs on the wart-like bumps, often coming from
    slightly raised bases.
    18 spot ladybird:- ground colour usually greyish brown
    on upper surface. Legs pale but dark at the end. The
    wart-like bumps bear few hairs, which usually come
    directly from the surface of the wart, not being on raised
    bases.]

14 Ab 4 m pale   15
 – Ab 4 m dark   21

15 Ab 4 o dark. (Ground colour greyish brown. Pronotum
    dark brown with broad pale brown or orange-brown
    oblique strip running from outer angle at front margin
    to centre line at back margin)
                           Adonis' ladybird (*Adonia variegata*)
 – Ab 4 o pale   16

16 Ab 4 i pale (like Ab 1 m and o and Ab 4 m and o).
    (Pronotum black with thin oblique greyish stripe
    running from front margin, just in from outer angle, to a
    point mid-way between the rear angle and the centre
    line on the hind margin)
                     13 spot ladybird (*Hippodamia 13-punctata*)
 – Ab 4 i dark   17

17 Prothorax with four plates. Dark markings on
    pronotum centre line and outer margin completely or
    almost completely separated by pale area, yellow,
    orange or reddish brown   18
 – Prothorax with two plates. Dark markings on pronotum
    continuous from centre line to outer margin   20

18 Ab 6–7 m orange or red
                          5 spot ladybird (*Coccinella 5-punctata*)
 – Ab 6–7 m black   19

19   Ab 1 and 4 o and m yellow, orange or red. Side of
     metathorax dark

                    7 spot ladybird (*Coccinella 7-punctata*)

  – Ab 1 and 4 o and m white, pale yellow or fawn. Side of
     metathorax pale

               Scarce 7 spot ladybird (*Coccinella magnifica*)

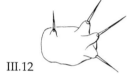

III.11

20   Ab 1 and 4 o and m white or off-white. Outer warts
     fairly densely covered with hairs on raised bases (III.11).
     Base of claw at the end of the legs has a well developed
     squarish tooth

           Hieroglyphic ladybird (*Coccinella hieroglyphica*)

III.12

  – Ab 1 and 4 o and m yellow. Outer warts sparsely
     covered with hairs on raised bases (III.12). Base of claw
     at the end of the legs without a squarish tooth

               11 spot ladybird (*Coccinella 11-punctata*)

21   Ab 4 o dark. (Ground colour greyish brown. Pronotum
     dark brown with broad pale brown or orange-brown
     oblique stripe running from outer angle at front margin
     to centre line at back margin)

                      Adonis' ladybird (*Adonia variegata*)

  – Ab 4 o pale   22

22   Ab 5,7,8 o pale. (Warts covered with hairs which are
     borne on raised bases. White or pale yellow mark
     centrally on Ab 4 inside Ab 4 i)

                     10 spot ladybird (*Adalia 10-punctata*)

  – Ab 5,7,8 o dark   23

23   Ab 6 o pale. Warts covered with hairs which are borne
     directly on the warts, not on raised bases

                  Striped ladybird (*Myzia oblongoguttata*)

  – Ab 6 o dark. Warts covered with hairs which are borne
     on raised bases. (Yellow-orange, orange or orange-red
     mark centrally on Ab 4 inside Ab 4 i)

                       2 spot ladybird (*Adalia 2-punctata*)

9 Study techniques and materials

9.1 Collecting techniques and equipment

Where to collect

Although ladybirds may be found in almost any terrestrial habitat in Britain, there is great variation in the number and variety that occur in different places. If a particular species is to be collected, then a suitable habitat and type of vegetation must be chosen (see chapter 3). But many studies involve species diversity in a particular area and the main problem is to ensure that the site is searched efficiently. The various techniques described below are useful for different types of vegetation. When they are combined, an area can be thoroughly investigated.

Searching, beating and sweeping

In many cases, all stages of the life cycle will be found by searching appropriate vegetation by eye. Adults and larvae can be picked up by pushing a paint brush under their legs, or by knocking them straight into a container. Eggs or pupae are easily damaged if removed from the substrate, so the leaf to which they are attached should be collected.

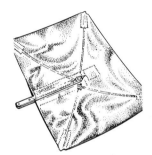

Fig. 37. Beating tray.

Collecting by eye is not always suitable or productive because some ladybirds are difficult to find due to their size, colour or habits. Some live on trees or bushes that are difficult to search, so a beating tray is a useful piece of equipment. This is a piece of white linen stretched over a wooden frame (fig. 37). Placed under branches or bushes that are given a few sharp taps with a stout stick, the tray will catch any ladybirds that fall out. (Care should be taken to avoid damaging the vegetation.)

Beating trays can be bought from entomological dealers, but a good substitute is an old umbrella held upside down under the foliage. White or pale material is best as the ladybirds are easy to see, but black will work if the debris in the umbrella is searched carefully.

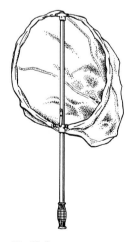

Fig. 38. Sweep net.

A sweep net is used for collecting in grasslands, on heaths, or from low growing vegetation. It is made from a white linen bag on a stout ring that is attached to a sturdy stick (fig. 38). It is used by walking slowly through the vegetation and sweeping the net from side to side. It is quite difficult and very time consuming to search low vegetation systematically, particularly if looking for small or less brightly marked species. However, by sweep-netting, considerable areas of vegetation can be covered in a short time. The technique is particularly useful for collecting the 16, 22 and 24 spot ladybirds in grass and meadowlands, and for finding the heather and hieroglyphic ladybirds in heather.

Sweep nets can also be bought from entomological dealers. However, they can be made very cheaply. Three pieces of heavy gauge wire about 140 cm long should be twisted together and bent into a circle of about 40 cm diameter. The excess pieces at the end are bent outwards and embedded into the end of a metre piece of 2.5 cm wood dowelling, or attached to the dowelling by a couple of jubilee clips once the net bag has been threaded onto the rim. The bag is made of strong white calico or canvas material with a hem wide enough for the wire to be threaded through. If you strengthen the hem with a strip of hessian the net bag will last considerably longer. The net bag should be 45 to 60 cm deep.

Containers for collecting ladybirds

Virtually any solid container with a secure lid can be used for collecting and storing ladybirds for a few hours. Transparent containers are better than opaque ones as the ladybirds can be seen, and plastic or perspex boxes tend to produce less condensation than glass jars. Clear perspex sandwich boxes are ideal. There is no need to worry about an air supply; even an airtight box will support a good number of ladybirds for many hours. If the ladybirds are likely to be kept in boxes for several hours, it is advisable to give them some food. This is particularly true of larvae because of their cannibalistic tendencies. Because ladybirds are normally found with colonies of aphids, providing food in the field is usually easy. It also helps if a few pieces of dead twig or grass are put into the boxes for the ladybirds to crawl about on, but green vegetation increases condensation. Tissue paper or kitchen towel laid flat in the base of the container will soak up the moisture and prevent drowning. Keeping boxes out of direct sunlight will also help reduce condensation. In fact, containers with ladybirds should never be left in direct sunlight, even for a few minutes, or the ladybirds will die from overheating.

Recording schemes

Anyone interested in ladybirds can become involved in one of the two main coccinellid recording schemes that collate records. The Natural Environment Research Council's

Biological Records Centre, at Monks Wood, is hoping to publish an atlas of British ladybird distributions in the near future. The atlas will be titled 'Coccinellidae Distribution Maps Scheme – Preliminary Distribution Maps'. Details of this scheme can be obtained from Dr J. Muggleton, Ministry of Agriculture, Fisheries and Food, Slough Laboratories, London Road, Slough, Berks SL3 7HJ. The second scheme, run by the Cambridge Ladybird Survey and incorporating the WATCH Ladybird Spot, was set up in 1984 by Dr M. Majerus in an attempt to obtain up-to-date and nationwide distribution data on British ladybirds. Details of this scheme can be obtained from Dr M.E.N. Majerus, Department of Genetics Field Station, 219d Huntingdon Road, Cambridge CB3 0DL.

9.2 Ladybird culturing techniques

The culturing techniques described below have been designed for the 2 spot ladybird. However, many other species may be bred successfully using these methods as they are, or with slight modifications (see p.87).

Housing ladybirds

Plastic petri dishes are the best breeding containers for ladybirds. A dish can hold a small population of about twenty 2 spot ladybirds, or species of a similar size. Large species such as the 7 spot or eyed ladybirds require more space, so a dish will only hold about ten individuals.

If a large population is required, the adults can be kept in several dishes. Alternatively, a plastic sandwich box can be used, but egg cannibalism can become common and it is not so easy to feed, clean and handle the population.

In some of our experimental work we have used large perspex cages, 2m x 1m x 1m, containing bean plants infested with aphids; but these require a great deal of attention to maintain the balance between beans, aphids and ladybirds. They are useful if very large cultures are kept, and for some population experiments, but they are not suitable for more general use.

The main task in breeding ladybirds is providing sufficient food. Most species are carnivores, and while we have not yet found a completely successful substitute for live prey, many species will breed successfully in the laboratory when fed on easily cultured aphid species that are not necessarily part of their natural diet.

The most successful method is to culture the pea aphid on broad beans. Cultures can be maintained all year round in a greenhouse by providing supplementary light and heat in the winter. Broad beans should be planted regularly to provide a constant supply. Eight seeds can be planted in a 12 cm pot. They take about a week to germinate and should be infected with aphids about two weeks later, when the plants are approximately 25 cm high. The beans will also need staking at about the same time. Aphids should be placed on the leaves at a density of about 40 per plant. They will multiply very rapidly and harvesting can begin after another week. This is done by brushing aphids from leaves and stems into a box held below.

Bean plants are easily damaged by heavy aphid infestations and begin to die back quite rapidly if the aphids get out of control or if the plants are not well watered. It is a matter of trial and error to decide how many aphids to remove each day to maintain a good supply, but production from one plant should last about two weeks.

Collecting wild aphids

Aphids can be obtained from wild or garden plants during the summer. Ladybirds survive and breed much better on some aphid species than on others. In fact, some aphids are poisonous and can even be fatal to ladybirds if eaten (see p. 20). The most useful guideline is that aphids are usually suitable as a food when ladybirds are found feeding on them in the wild. The plants on which aphids are found vary from month to month and with the weather. Those which carry large aphid populations in one year do not always do so the next. Good sources of aphids are often found on garden roses, sweet peas, thistles, and knapweed, as well as apple, lime, sycamore and willow trees. But nettles are the most consistent source. The aphids can be collected by brushing them from the leaves into a perspex sandwich box, and nettles are no problem if gloves are worn.

When using wild aphids, there is a danger of contaminating laboratory stocks with wild ladybird larvae and other organisms which can be a nuisance in ladybird cultures. These include various hoverfly or lacewing larvae, as well as small spiders. All these should be removed from cultures.

Feeding ladybirds

The number of aphids given to ladybirds each day will depend on the size of aphid and ladybird species, but about 15–20 full-grown pea aphids per day are sufficient to keep a pair of 2 spots breeding successfully. Aphids can be transferred by using a small paint brush. With a bit of practice it becomes very easy to pick up not only aphids, but also the ladybirds themselves.

Alternative and artificial diets

A useful alternative to live aphids are deep frozen ones. Aphids collected in the summer should be placed directly into a deep freezer in a sandwich box or similar container. Ladybirds will feed on deep frozen aphids provided that these were alive when frozen. But the aphids should not be thawed and refrozen too often, as they soon become reduced to an unmanageable mess. So only the number required should be removed from the freezer when feeding.

There are many descriptions in the literature of foods which are alternatives to live prey. These are either crude preparations such as chopped banana, liver or honey, or fairly sophisticated artificial diets such as the one described below (see Henderson and Albrecht, in press). There is no substitute for live food for maintaining stocks in breeding condition, but some of the alternatives can keep adults alive for relatively long periods. They should not be used for larvae as mortality increases rapidly. The only crude preparation which can be recommended is chopped banana. This can be useful but it has to be cut into very small pieces and it must be replaced every day.

The artificial diet we use is as follows:

Ingredients

6 grams yeast (dried, powdered and ground)
9 grams commercially available powdered and
    desiccated liver
15 grams sugar
10 ml maple syrup (pure)
2-3 Boots vitamin pills (without iron or copper)
    ground to a powder
2 grams agar
150 ml water

Method

Grind the yeast, liver and sugar in a pestle and
    mortar or a glass Pyrex bowl.
Separately crush the vitamin pills, and put to one side.
Dissolve agar in 150 ml water in a large 500 ml
    bottle in a microwave oven, or in a small
    saucepan or Pyrex bowl on a hot ring or

bunsen. Pour into the receptacle containing the powdered ingredients and mix thoroughly. Reheat in microwave or over a hot ring or bunsen until the solids are dispersed evenly.

Allow to cool to approximately 50°C, then add the crushed vitamin pills and maple syrup and stir until cool enough to pour. Pour into petri dishes, or other containers, cover and allow to cool.

Store in a fridge.

The artificial food will keep for about a week in a fridge. After this time it may develop fungal and bacterial growths. Large quantities can be made and stored in a deep freeze, but the medium is never as good when it has been frozen and thawed.

The artificial food is prepared by slicing it, in the petri dish, into small blocks about 4mm square. A block can then be lifted from the dish with forceps and placed into the ladybird dish. A block of this size is sufficient for about five ladybirds. The artificial medium should be replaced each day.

Care of eggs, larvae and pupae

Many ladybird species mate and lay eggs if they are kept in suitable containers with plenty of food. The eggs are usually laid on the inside surface of the petri dish. They are easily damaged and ladybirds often eat their own eggs, particularly if they are short of aphids. So the parents should be separated from their eggs as soon as possible. It is a good idea to transfer the ladybirds to a fresh petri dish each day even when no eggs have been laid. Clean containers increase the frequency of mating and egg-laying. Plastic petri dishes can be used many times, provided they are washed in warm clean water.

Petri dishes containing eggs should be kept at room temperature. Eggs of most species hatch within four to seven days. Those which have not hatched after about ten days are probably infertile; they tend to shrink and become a dirty yellow or orange colour, and they can be discarded. When a fertile egg hatches, the young larva crawls out, and its first meal is the egg shell. It will also feed on any surrounding infertile eggs that have not hatched. Newly emerged larvae should not be moved as they are easily damaged.

Larvae should be supplied with live aphids daily from the time that they hatch. It is not necessary to transfer larvae to fresh containers each day, but if many larvae hatch in one dish, it is advisable to move some to another dish because of their cannibalistic tendencies. If there is a shortage of aphid food, larvae soon resort to eating each other. And it is difficult to keep a dish containing more than ten larvae beyond the second instar fully stocked with aphids the whole time.

Viral and bacterial infections can be a problem in ladybird cultures and they are usually highly infectious. Petri dishes should be kept as clean as possible to prevent disease. Larvae are particularly vulnerable and it is best to brush out the debris of dead aphids regularly. In addition, all unhealthy or dead larvae should be discarded immediately, and it is often worth disposing of an entire dish, even if some of the larvae appear healthy. If an infected dish contains some apparently healthy larvae that are particularly important, these larvae should be removed to a clean dish with a paint brush. This dish should then be physically separated from healthy stocks. Dishes and brushes which have been in contact with infected stocks should be disinfected in methylated spirits.

The larvae of the 2 spot feed up in about three weeks when kept at room temperature with a good supply of aphids. They usually pupate on the sides of the dishes and then emerge about a week later. Moulting or pupating larvae, and newly emerged adults, should never be disturbed.

The 2 spot will breed continuously throughout the year if kept warm with a constant supply of aphids. It is possible to get six or more generations a year. It should be noted, however, that newly emerged adults tend not to mate until they have been out of the pupa for about a week.

Culturing other species of British ladybirds

The techniques we have described for the 2 spot can be used for many other British species, although minor modifications are sometimes necessary. Using these methods we have successfully bred most of the species listed in table 14 through at least a full generation. Table 14 also contains notes on whether the species will continuously brood in the laboratory, and if not, when egg-laying adults may be collected. Modifications to the basic 2 spot regime are suggested, when necessary, to improve the culture for a particular species.

Two of the carnivorous species seem very difficult to breed in captivity. The hieroglyphic ladybird probably

Table 14. *Notes on breeding and rearing carnivorous British ladybirds*

10 spot ladybird 14 spot ladybird 5 spot ladybird Adonis' ladybird Cream-streaked ladybird Cream-spot ladybird Water ladybird 13 spot ladybird	As 2 spot.
7 spot ladybird Scarce 7 spot ladybird 11 spot ladybird	Continuously brood, need very large numbers of aphids, adults dislike artificial food.
Eyed ladybird 18 spot ladybird	Will not continuously brood, require period of increasing day length to promote mating and egg-laying. Mated females may be collected from March to June. Larvae need excess of aphids as they are highly cannibalistic.
Pine ladybird	Will not continuously brood, requires period of increasing day length to promote mating and egg-laying. Mated females may be collected from February to June.
Larch ladybird	Continuously broods, will tolerate large amounts of artificial food in place of aphids with little reduction in egg-laying. Egg-laying can be increased by placing a few pine needles in the petri dish.
Heather ladybird Kidney-spot ladybird	Continuously brood, but at a low rate. We suspect improvements could be made for these species. Breeds better when fed on smaller aphid species or scale insects.
Striped ladybird	Females fail to lay eggs unless fed on aphids from pine. Larvae may develop on other species of aphid, such as pea aphids, but there is high mortality. Mated females may be collected from March to June.
Hieroglyphic ladybird	We have been unable to induce mating or oviposition in captivity. Wild caught larvae will develop normally if fed on pea aphids.

needs the specific species of prey on which it feeds on heather to induce egg-laying. It will feed on various species of aphid in captivity, but fails to lay eggs. The striped ladybird readily mates in captivity, but again will not lay eggs unless it is fed on its natural food, in this case several species of pine aphid. If gravid females are brought into captivity from the wild in the spring, they will lay fertile eggs for a few days, but egg laying decreases quickly if they are not given their natural food.

Non-carnivorous ladybirds

The vegetarian and three mildew feeding species present particular problems for breeding in captivity. Two of them, the 24 spot and 22 spot, we have been able to breed successfully. The vegetarian 24 spot is not too difficult if fresh leaves of suitable plants are provided for adults and larvae every day. Similarly, the mildew feeding 22 spot can be bred if sections of leaves of hogweed, wild angelica or some similar species, with a good dusting of powdery mildew, are provided daily. The other two species of mildew feeders, the 16 spot and orange ladybirds, we have not been able to breed. We suspect that they require particular species of mildew to promote mating and oviposition. All four of these species will readily feed on artificial food and although they will not mate or lay eggs, they can be kept alive for many months solely on this diet.

9.3 Study techniques

Making a collection

If it is necessary to kill ladybirds for study or for a collection, this may be done by placing the ladybirds in a killing jar, or a corked glass tube, into the bottom of which about 1 cm of dental plaster or filter paper has been set to absorb the killing fluid. Ethyl acetate is probably the best killing agent, although chloroform, diethyl ether or carbon tetrachloride can also be used. Put a few drops of ethyl acetate onto the absorbent material and try to avoid inhaling too much of the vapour yourself.

When dead the ladybirds should be pinned fairly quickly as they become brittle as they dry out. There are two ways of pinning or setting ladybirds. One is the way normally used for setting beetles. Here the ladybird is mounted on a small rectangular piece of stiff white card. A small drop of gum (powdered gum tragacanth with a drop of water is usually used by entomologists, but wallpaper glue or PVC gum are alternatives) is placed on the card, and

Fig. 39. Ladybird mounted on card with a data label below.

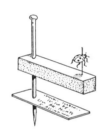

Fig. 40. Ladybird mounted on a thin headless pin, in turn mounted on polyporus pith, set on a robust pin, with a data label below.

the ladybird is set on this with the legs and antennae spread out (fig. 39). The card is then supported on a stainless steel entomological pin. These can be obtained from entomological dealers in different lengths and thicknesses. Carding has the disadvantage that the underparts of ladybirds set in this way can no longer be examined. The other method is direct pinning, whereby an entomological pin is passed straight through the insect. A collection looks neater if the pins are always passed through the insect at roughly the same point. Usually, a point just to the right of the central line and just behind the pronotum is chosen. For smaller species of coccinellids one uses thin headless entomological pins, or short fine pins, which in turn are mounted on a strip of plastazote or polyporus pith set on a long robust pin for ease of handling (fig. 40).

All set specimens should have a data label placed on the main pin below the insect. The information on data labels varies, but must include date and location of capture, with county and preferably grid reference. Other information that may be added on the same or another label includes the species name with the initials of the identifier, the sex of the specimen, details of the plant or situation in which the ladybird was found, the weather conditions, what the ladybird was doing (if relevant), and the name or initials of the collector. When specimens have come from wild caught immature stages which have been bred up in captivity, the stage in which the insect was originally taken should be recorded (e.g. ex larva). The dates of pupation and emergence may also be recorded. If all this information will not fit on small neat labels under the insect, then as long as the location and date are recorded on a data label, a second label giving simply a specimen number can be added to the pin. Other information for that particular specimen number can then be given in a data book.

Set ladybirds should be kept in cork-lined wooden insect store boxes. Because dried insects are prone to attack by mites and museum beetles, a repellent, such as naphthalene or paradichlorobenzene crystals, should be placed in the box, securely pinned down in a twist of paper so that free crystals cannot knock against the specimens.

A collection of larvae can be made, by placing them in 70% alcohol which will kill and preserve them, although they will lose their natural colouration. The colours of the larvae will be maintained better if larval skins are emptied and blown, or freeze dried. However, both these techniques are rather difficult and time consuming, and require specialist equipment. A set of good close-up colour photographs provides an excellent alternative, and avoids the need to kill larvae.

Basic examination

Most ladybirds can be identified fairly easily and a hand lens is rarely needed. For convenience of examination under a microscope, a ladybird is best anaesthetised by squirting into its container a dose of carbon dioxide from a sparklet operated wine bottle opener. When looking closely at the anatomy of ladybirds it is often worth drawing what you see, in order to keep a clear record of your observations. Drawing the structures also ensures that you examine specimens closely. In order to draw fine detail accurately and to scale, it is helpful to use a microscope that has a grid graticule in one of the eye pieces, and to use a sheet of paper which has been lightly ruled into squares. Or use a microscope with a fitted drawing attachment.

Examining genitalia

The genitalia of insects are important in identification, and for this reason they are also of interest in ladybirds. The male genitalia are most commonly investigated, but they are small so it is necessary to study them mounted on a slide under a microscope (fig. 41).

The best way to prepare a male genitalia slide is to remove the final third of the abdomen and place it in a 10% solution of potassium hydroxide for 24 hours to dissolve the soft parts. This process can be helped by gently heating the solution. The specimen should be placed in pure glacial acetic acid for five minutes. It is then washed in water, and dehydrated by passing it through a series of alcohols of increasing concentration and then removed to clove oil. It should finally be arranged with fine needles and mounted in Canada balsam to make it permanent. Alternatively, after soaking in glacial acetic acid and washing in water, the specimen may be immediately mounted in Berlese fluid or polyvinyl lactophenol.

Other parts of ladybirds can be examined in the same way. The mouthparts of both adults and larvae can be of particular interest, and so can adult wing venation patterns. For further details of how to make slide preparations of anatomical structures of beetles, see the Amateur Entomologists' Society's book *A Coleopterist's Handbook* (Walsh and Dibb, 1975).

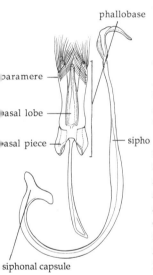

phallobase

paramere

basal lobe

basal piece

sipho

siphonal capsule

Fig. 41. Male genitalia.

Chromosome preparations

It is not possible to give a comprehensive guide to making chromosome preparations in this book, but for those with the facilities Darlington and La Cour's (1960) book *Handling Chromosomes* will help. The basic method is to dissect out the male testes and place them in a drop of fixing solution (one part glacial acetic acid to three parts absolute alcohol) on a microscope slide. They should then be gently macerated. After a few minutes a drop of staining solution (2% orcein in 50% glacial acetic acid) is added and left for about ten minutes. The material is then covered with a coverslip and squashed by placing the slide between some pieces of filter paper or tissue and applying firm pressure with the ball of the thumb. The slide can then be examined with a microscope.

sex chromosome: a chromosome which is present in a reproductive cell (or gamete) and which carries the factor for producing a male or female offspring. Such chromosomes are usually denoted by the letters X and Y. In humans (and most ladybirds) females carry two X chromosomes, and males carry one X and one Y chromosome

metaphase: a stage in cell division in which the pairs of chromosomes are arranged along the equator of the cell nucleus

Most ladybird species have a characteristic set of ten pairs of small chromosomes. The only unusual features are the sex chromosomes which in males appear as a curious structure at the metaphase stage of cell division. This is known as an XYp, because the tiny Y chromosome is bound together with the larger X, giving the impression of a man dangling on a parachute.

Some species have a completely different chromosome complement from the standard ladybird type. The cream-streaked ladybird has only eight pairs of chromosomes: six normal pairs, one very large pair, which seem to be the product of fusions between three normal pairs, and an XYp sex chromosome pair. The eyed ladybird has nine pairs of relatively large chromosomes. It has a neo-XY sex chromosome system in which the Y chromosome has been transferred to an autosome. The heather ladybird also has a neo-XY sex chromosome system, but has ten other pairs giving eleven pairs in all. The pine ladybird is interesting because it has only seven pairs including a neo-XY system, and because some populations also have B chromosomes in addition to the normal complement. Most British populations are polymorphic for presence or absence of a long B chromosome. In a few populations, a second, small B chromosome may be present (Henderson, in press). The distribution and frequency of these chromosomes is unknown for most of the populations in the UK. Finally, the larch ladybird has the normal chromosome complement except that it lacks the Y chromosome, so while females have 20 chromosomes (nine normal pairs and two X sex chromosomes), males have just 19 chromosomes (nine pairs, and one X chromosome).

Electrophoresis

Gel electrophoresis is a technique which has been widely used for estimating genetic variation in natural populations.

It detects variations in proteins which are encoded by genes. The process involves placing ground up tissue from several individuals into a gel, usually made of starch. An electric current is applied to the gel and the proteins migrate at different rates depending on their overall charge and molecular size.

When the gel is removed from the current, specific proteins can be detected by applying a suitable stain. If samples from several individuals are placed side by side their migration rates can be compared. Differences between individuals are very often due to genetic variation. So, if one compares a number of different proteins, it is possible to estimate the level of genetic variation in populations. It is also possible to compare different species by this technique which can be an aid to taxonomic and phylogenetic studies. Many texts have been written about electrophoretic techniques and their use. Brewer's (1970) *An Introduction to Isozyme Techniques* gives a good general account.

Mark release and recapture

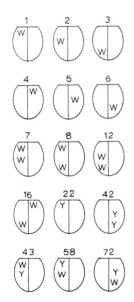

For many population and behavioural studies on adult ladybirds a technique called mark-release-recapture is used. Samples of ladybirds are caught, anaesthetised and marked using a quick-drying cellulose paint (Humbrol model aeroplane dope or Tippex are suitable). A tiny spot is carefully applied to the elytra with a fine paint brush, or with the end of a cocktail stick. The marked ladybirds should be kept under careful observation until the paint has dried to ensure that they do not get gummed up. When the paint is dry and the ladybirds have recovered from the anaesthetic they can be released where desired. For some behavioural studies it may be necessary to mark each ladybird with a different mark so that they can be individually recognised again. By placing one or two spots on specific points on the elytra and using different combinations of coloured paints, a large number of different marks can be produced. For example, using six different positions (see fig. 42) on the elytra and a combination of one or two spots of two colours, 72 different pattern markings can be produced. If three colours are used this number is increased to 153. These can be used to differentiate between insects marked on different dates, on different host plants, in different habitats and so on. The marking pattern assigned to a particular ladybird, together with the details about it relevant to a particular study, should be recorded in a log-book.

Fig. 42. Marking patterns for individual recognition of 72 ladybirds by use of six elytra positions and two colours (white = W, yellow = Y) employed separately or in combination. (With 3 colours, 153 combinations are possible.)

Repeated captures and releases over a period of time can provide information on population size, migration, rate of emergence of adults from pupae, mortality, life span, sex ratios, and the habits of individual ladybirds.

Even by the most stringent searching and sampling it is rare to find all the individuals of a species in a particular area. More usually, only a proportion will be marked, in which case the Lincoln Index formula can be used to estimate the total population size:

total population = total number collected in second sample x number marked in first sample ÷ number of marked specimens recaptured.

For example, in 1985 a first sample of 800 pine ladybirds were captured and marked and released. In a second sample of 600 pine ladybirds captured a week later, 30 had been marked.

Total estimated population $= \dfrac{600 \times 800}{30} = 16\,000$

(The 95% confidence limits of the estimation of population size are given as

$$N \pm 2N\sqrt{\frac{1}{R} - \frac{1}{S_2}}$$

where   N = estimated population size
         R = number of marked individuals recaptured
and S_2 = total number in second sample

The 95% confidence limit range is the range of population sizes, given random sampling error, within which one could be 95% certain that the true population size lies. Put another way, there is only a one in 20 chance that the real population size does not fall within this range.)

The formula for estimating population size involves a number of assumptions: (1) that the population remains constant between samples (that is, no new ladybirds enter the population, and none die or leave it); (2) that all individuals have an equal chance of being captured; (3) that marked individuals are not more or less likely to be captured; and (4) that a reasonable number of marked individuals are captured in the second sample. The time interval between marking and recapture should be long enough to allow thorough mixing of marked individuals with the others (assumption 3) but not long enough to allow much migration or mortality (assumption 1). In practice the ideal interval to use with ladybirds varies with the time of year, weather conditions and their food supply, but, except in winter when ladybirds move little, a week is usually suitable. For more details of the methods of analysis relating to mark-release-recapture studies and for details of more sophisticated population size techniques, such as multiple capture-recapture and removal sampling, Chalmers and Parker's (1986) *OU Project Guide*, Begon's (1979) *Investigating Animal Abundance* or Blower, Cook and Bishop's (1981) *Estimating the size of animal populations* may be consulted.

How to present your findings

Writing up is an important part of any research project, particularly when the findings are to be communicated to other people. A thorough, critical investigation that has produced novel results and new information of general interest should be published. Journals that publish short papers on insect biology include the *Bulletin of the Amateur Entomologists' Society, Entomologists' Monthly Magazine, Entomologist's Gazette, Entomologists' Record and Journal of Variation* and the *British Journal of Entomology and Natural History*. For material with an educational slant the *Journal of Biological Education* is very good. Those unfamiliar with publishing conventions are advised to examine current numbers of these journals to see what sort of articles they publish. It is then time to consult an appropriate expert who can give advice on whether and in what form the material might be published. Then write the paper, following the normal format for the journal and keeping it as short as you can, while still presenting enough information to establish the conclusions. Diagrams are often a useful means of expressing data and these should be clear and accurate. It is an unbreakable rule of scientific publication that results are reported with scrupulous honesty. Hence it is essential to keep detailed and accurate records throughout the investigation, and to distinguish in the write-up between certainty and probability, and between deduction and speculation. In many cases it will be necessary to apply appropriate statistical techniques to test the significance of findings. A book such as Bailey's (1959) *Statistical Methods in Biology*, Parker's (1973) *Introductory Statistics for Biology*, or Chalmers and Parker's (1986) *OU Project Guide* will help, but this is an area where expert advice can contribute much to the planning, as well as to the analysis, of the work.

Further reading

Finding books

Some of the books and journals listed here will be unavailable in local and school libraries. It is possible to make arrangements to see or to borrow such works by seeking permission to visit the library of a local university, or by asking your local public library to borrow the work (or a photocopy of it) for you via the British Library, Document Supply Centre. This may take several weeks, and it is important to present your librarian with a reference which is correct in every detail. References are acceptable in the form and order given here, namely the author's name and date of publication, followed by (for a book) the title and publisher or (for a journal article) the title of the article, the journal title, the volume number and the first and last pages of the article.

References

Bailey, N.T.J. (1959). *Statistical Methods in Biology*. London: English Universities Press.
Banks, C.J. (1957). The behaviour of individual Coccinellid larvae on plants. *British Journal of Animal Behaviour*, **5**, 12-24.
Begon, M. (1979). *Investigating Animal Abundance: Capture-Recapture for Biologists*. London: Edward Arnold.
Benham, B.R. and Muggleton, J. (1970). Studies on the ecology of *Coccinella undecimpunctata* Linn. (Col. Coccinellidae). *Entomologist*, **103**, 153-170.
Blackman, R.L. (1965). Studies on specificity in Coccinellidae. *Annals of Applied Biology*, **56**, 336-338.
Blackman, R.L. (1967). The effects of different aphid foods on *Adalia bipunctata* L. and *Coccinella 7-punctata* L. *Annals of Applied Biology*, **59**, 207-219.
Blower, J.G., Cook, L.M. and Bishop, J.A. (1981). *Estimating the Size of Animal Populations*. London: Allen and Unwin.
Brakefield, P. (1985a). Differential winter mortality and seasonal selection in the polymorphic ladybird *Adalia bipunctata* in the Netherlands. *Biological Journal of the Linnean Society*, **24**, 189-206.
Brakefield, P. (1985b). Polymorphic Müllerian mimicry and interactions with thermal melanism in ladybirds and a soldier beetle: a hypothesis. *Biological Journal of the Linnean Society*, **26**, 243-267.
Brewer, G.J. (1970). *An Introduction to Isozyme Techniques*. New York and London: Academic Press.
Chalmers, N. and Parker, P. (1986). *OU Project Guide: Field Work and Statistics for Ecological Projects*. London: Open University/Field Studies Council.
Chinery, M. (1976). *A Field Guide to the Insects of Britain and Northern Europe*. London: Collins.
Creed, E.R. (1971). Melanism in the two-spot ladybird, *Adalia bipunctata*, in Great Britain. In *Ecological Genetics and Evolution* (ed. E.R. Creed), 134-151. Oxford: Blackwell Scientific Publications.
Crowson, R.A. (1956). *Coleoptera: Introduction and Keys to Families*. Royal Entomological Society of London, *Handbooks for the Identification of British Insects IV* (1), 1-59.

Darlington, C.P. and La Cour, L.F. (1960). *The Handling of Chromosomes* (3rd edition). London: Allen and Unwin.

Disney, R.H.L. (1983). *Scuttle-flies. Diptera: Phoridae (except* Megaselia*).* Royal Entomological Society of London *Handbooks for the Identification of British Insects. X(6)*, 1-81.

Dixon, A.G.F. (1958). The escape responses shown by certain aphids to the presence of the coccinellid *Adalia decempunctata* (L.). *Transactions of the Royal Entomological Society of London*, **110**, 319-334.

Dixon, A.G.F. (1959). An experimental study of the searching behaviour of the predatory coccinellid *Adalia decempunctata* (L.). *Journal of Animal Ecology*, **39**, 739-751.

Dobrzhanskii, F.G. (Dobzhansky, Th. G.) (1922a). Imaginal diapause in Coccinellidae. *Izv. Otd. prikl. Ent.*, **2**, 103-124.

Dobrzhanskii, F.G. (Dobzhansky, Th. G.) (1922b). Mass aggregations and migrations in Coccinellidae. *Izv. Otd. prikl. Ent.*, **2**, 229-234.

Donisthorpe, H. St. J.K. (1939). *A Preliminary list of the Coleoptera of Windsor Forest.* London.

Eastop, V.F. and Pope, R.D. (1969). Notes on the biology of some British Coccinellidae. *Entomologist*, **102**, 162-164.

El-Ziady, S. and Kennedy, J.S. (1956). Beneficial effects of the common garden ant, *Lasius niger* L. on the black bean aphid, *Aphis fabae* Scopoli. *Proceedings of the Royal Entomological Society of London, (A)*, **31**, 61-65.

van Emden, F.I. (1942). Key to the British families of beetle larvae, for ready identification. *Entomologists' Monthly Magazine*, **78**, 210-226 and 253-272.

van Emden, F.I. (1949). Larvae of British beetles. VII (Coccinellidae). *Entomologists' Monthly Magazine*, **85**, 265-283.

Evans, A.F. (1976a). The role of predator size ratio in determining the efficiency of capture by *Anthocoris nemorum* and the escape reactions of the prey, *Acyrthosiphum pisum*. *Ecological Entomology*, **1**, 85-90.

Evans, A.F. (1976b). The searching behaviour of *Anthocoris confusus* (Reuter) in relation to prey density and plant surface topography. *Ecological Entomology*, **1**, 163-169.

Feltwell, J. (1984). *Reader's Digest Guide to the Butterflies and other Insects of Britain.* London: Reader's Digest Association.

Frazer, J.F.D. and Rothschild, M. (1962). Defense mechanisms in warningly coloured moths and other insects. *11th International Congress of Entomology Vienna 1960B*, **3**, 249-256.

Harde, K.W. (1984). *A Field Guide in Colour to Beetles.* London: Octopus Books.

Hariri, G.E. (1966). Laboratory studies on the reproduction of *Adalia bipunctata* (Coleoptera, Coccinellidae). *Entomologia Experimentalis et Applicata*, **9**, 200-204.

Henderson, S.A. (1988). A correlation between B chromosome frequency and sex ratio in *Exochomus quadripustulatus*. *Chromosoma* (in press).

Henderson, S.A. and Albrecht, J.S. (1988). An artificial diet for maintaining ladybirds. *Entomologist's Record and Journal of Variation*, (in press).

Hodek, I. (1973). *Biology of Coccinellidae.* The Hague; Junk, Prague: Acad. Sci.

Iablokoff-Khnzorian, S.M. (1981). *Coleopteres-Coccinellidae. Tribu Coccinellini des regions Palaearctique et Orientale.* Paris: Boubee.

Ibrahim, M.M. (1955a). Studies on *Coccinella undecimpunctata aegyptiaca* Reiche. I. Preliminary notes and morphology of the early stages. *Bulletin of the Society of Entomologists Egypt*, **39**, 251-274.

Ibrahim, M.M. (1955b). Studies on *Coccinella undecimpunctata aegyptiaca* Reiche. II. Biology and life-history. *Bulletin of the Society of Entomologists Egypt*, **39**, 395-423.

Iperti, G. (1966). Comportment naturel des Coccinelles aphidiphages du Sud-Est de la France. Leur type de specificité, leur action predatrice sur *Aphis fabae* L. *Entomophaga*, **11**, 203-210.

Ireland, H., Kearns, P.W.E. and Majerus, M.E.N. (1986). Interspecific hybridisation in the Coccinellidae: some observations on an old controversy. *Entomologist's Record and Journal of Variation* **98**, 181-185.

Joy, N.M. (1932). *A Practical Handbook of British Beetles*. 2 vols. London: Witherby. (Reprint, E.W. Classey 1976).

Klingauf, F. (1967). Abwehr-und Meideraktionen von Blattlausen (Aphididae) bei Bedrohung durch Raubern und Parasiten. *Zeitschrift für angewandte Zoologie*, **60**, 269-317.

Komai, T. (1956). Genetics of lady-beetles. *Advances in Genetics*, **8**, 155-185.

Lane, C. and Rothschild, M. (1960). Notes on wasps visiting a mercury vapour trap, together with some observations on their behaviour towards their prey. *Entomologists' Monthly Magazine*, **95**, 277-279.

Linssen, E.F. (1959). *Beetles of the British Isles*. 2 vols. London: Warne.

Lusis, J.J. (1961). On the biological meaning of colour polymorphism of ladybeetle *Adalia bipunctata* L. *Latvijas Entomologs*, **4**, 3-29.

Mader, L. (1926-1937). *Evidenz der Palaarktischen Coccinelliden und ihrer Aberationen in Wort und Bild*. Vienna.

Majerus, M.E.N. (1985). Some notes on ladybirds from an acid heath. *Bulletin of the Amateur Entomologists' Society*, **45**, 31-37.

Majerus, M.E.N., Ireland, H. and Kearns, P.W.E. (1987). Description of a new form of *Adalia bipunctata* with notes on its inheritance. *Entomologist's Record and Journal of Variation*, **99**, 255-257.

Majerus, M.E.N., O'Donald, P., Kearns, P.W.E. and Ireland, H. (1986). The genetics and evolution of female choice. *Nature*, London, **321**, 164-167.

Majerus, M.E.N., O'Donald, P. and Weir, J. (1982a). Evidence for preferential mating in *Adalia bipunctata*. *Heredity*, **49**, 171-177.

Majerus, M.E.N., O'Donald, P. and Weir, J. (1982b). Female mating preference is genetic. *Nature*, London, **300**, 521-523.

Mayr, E. (1963). *Animal Species and Evolution*. Cambridge: Harvard University Press.

Moon, A. (1986). *Ladybirds in Dorset*. Dorchester: Dorset Environmental Records Centre.

Muggleton, J., Lonsdale, D. and Benham, B.R. (1975). Melanism in *Adalia bipunctata* L. (Col., Coccinellidae) and its relationship to atmospheric pollution. *Journal of Applied Ecology*, **23**, 101-111.

Muggleton, J. (1978). Selection against the melanic morphs of *Adalia bipunctata* (two spot ladybird): a review and some new data. *Heredity*, **40**, 269-280.

Parker, R.E. (1973). *Introductory Statistics for Biology* (Studies in Biology). London: Edward Arnold.

Pontin, A.J. (1960). Some records of predators and parasites adapted to attack aphids attended by ants. *Entomologists' Monthly Magazine*, **95**, 154.

Pope, R.D. (1953). *Coccinellidae and Sphindidae*. Royal Entomological Society of London, *Handbooks for the identification of British Insects* V(7).

Pope, R.D. (1973). The species of *Scymnus* (s. str.), *Scymnus* (*Pullus*) and *Nephus* (Col., Coccinellidae) occurring in the British Isles. *Entomologists' Monthly Magazine*, **109**, 3-39.

Rotheray, G. (1989). *Aphid Predators*. Naturalists' Handbooks, 11, Richmond Publishing Co. Ltd.

Rothschild, M. (1961). Defensive odours and Müllerian mimicry among insects. *Transactions of the Royal Entomological Society of London*, **113**, 101-122.

Scali, V. and Creed, E.R. (1975). The influence of climate on melanism in the two-spot ladybird, *Adalia bipunctata*, in central Italy. *Transactions of the Royal Entomological Society of London*, **127**, 163-169.

Sem'yanov, V.P. (1970). Biological properties of *Adalia bipunctata* L. (Coleoptera, Coccinellidae) in conditions of Leningrad region. *Zashch. Rast. Vredit Bolez.*, **127**, 105-112.

Skidmore, P. (1985). *Exochomus nigromaculatus* (Goeze) (Col., Coccinellidae) in Britain. *Entomologists' Monthly* Magazine, **121**, 239-240.

Stephens, J.F. (1831–2). *Illustrations of British Entomology. Mandibulata*, 4. London.

Sundby, R.A. (1966). A comparative study of the efficiency of three predatory insects - *Coccinella septempunctata* L. (Coleoptera, Coccinellidae), *Chrysopa carnea* St. (Neuroptera, Chrysopidae) and *Syrphus ribesii* L. (Diptera, Syrphidae) at two different temperatures. *Entomophaga*, **11**, 395-404.

Timofeeff-Ressovsky, N.W. (1940). Zur analyse des Polymorphismus bei *Adalia bipunctata* L. *Biologisches Zentralblatt*, **60**, 130-137.

Unwin, D. (1984). A key to the families of British Coleoptera (and Strepsiptera). *Field Studies*, **6**, 149-197. An AIDGAP key.

Walsh, G.B. and Dibb, J.R. (1975). *A Coleopterist's Handbook* (2nd edition, revised). London: Amateur Entomologists' Society.

Useful addresses

Ladybird recording schemes

Dr M.E.N. Majerus, The Cambridge Ladybird Survey, Department of Genetics Field Station, 219d Huntingdon Road, Cambridge CB3 ODL.

Dr J. Muggleton, Coccinellidae Distribution Mapping Scheme, c/o Ministry of Agriculture, Fisheries and Food, Slough Laboratories, London Road, Slough, Berks SL3 7HJ.

Entomological equipment suppliers

Watkins and Doncaster, Four Throws, Hawkhurst, Kent.

Worldwide Butterflies Ltd., Compton House, nr. Sherborne, Dorset DT9 4QN.

Suppliers of entomological books, new and secondhand

E.W. Classey Ltd., P.O.Box 93, Farringdon, Oxon SN7 7DR.

L. Christie, 129 Franciscan Road, Tooting, London SW17 8DZ.

Wyseby House Books, Oxdrove, Burghclere, Newbury, Berkshire RG15 9JS.

Entomological and other societies

Amateur Entomologists' Society, 8 Heather Close, New Haw, Weybridge, Surrey KT15 3PF.

British Entomological and Natural History Society, c/o The Alpine Club, 74 South Audley Street, London WIY 5FF.

Royal Entomological Society of London, 41 Queen's Gate, London SW7 5HV.

WATCH Trust for Environmental Education, 22 The Green, Nettleham, Lincoln LN2 2NR.

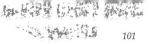

Index

Throughout the text (with the exception of the keys in chapter 8), English names of ladybirds are used, rather than the scientific names. Mentions of ladybirds are thus generally indexed under English names. A listing of the scientific names of the British ladybirds, with their English equivalents, is given in table 1, on page 3. English names that begin with a numeral are indexed as though numerals are written in full (e.g. 7 spot ladybird is indexed under s).